MW00510334

ISBN: 978-1-54396-418-9
ISBN eBook: 978-1-54396-419-6

We hope our story will warm your heart & encourage you to practice gratitude!

THE STROKE THAT TOUCHED MY *Heart*

How Gratitude Transformed a 37 Year-Old Massive Stroke Survivor

In gratitude!

MIA & MYRTLE RUSSELL

Mia & Myrtle

Introduction...1
Intuition...4
Emergency Rooms (ER)...9
Prayer...14
Hope...17
Diagnostic Tests...18
A Craniectomy...19
A Neurosurgeon's "Piece of Cake"...21
Joy...24
Good Luck Charms...26
Insurance...29
Helmets...30
Encouraging Words...31
The World Wide Web...32
Classmates...34
Vigilance...35
A Time To Search...37
Home Remedies...38
Laughter ...40
Big Brothers ...41
A Dying Friend...43
Answers...45
Social Security Disability Benefits...46
Student Loans ...47

Taxes...48
Assistive Devices...49
Valentines...50
Jigsaw Puzzles ...52
Disappointment...53
Resources...55
Social Workers...56
Goodbyes...57
Motorized Shopping Carts...59
Acts of Kindness...60
Outpatient Therapists...61
Mix-Matched Shoes...62
"Thank You" Notes...63
A Shower...64
Remembering the Stroke...65
Learning To Write My Name...67
Medical Bills and Bad Credit...68
Choices...69
Co-Workers...71
Change...72
Her Daddy's Genes...73
Reflections...74
Neuroplasticity...77
Patience...79
Fear...80
A Hard-Headed Fall...81
$6 Glasses...82
Sisters...83
Is Age More Than A Number?...85
A Center for the Disabled...86
Bedtime Stories...88

Smart Phones...89

A Fanny Pack...90

Good News...91

Gratitude Journaling...92

A Seizure ...93

Something to Sing About...96

Birds On The Line...98

Closed Doors and Opened Windows...99

Supplemental Security Income...100

Good Grief!...101

Baby Steps...103

Mothers...105

Medicaid...106

Bonds...107

Anger...109

A Gratitude Story...111

Anticipation...112

A Good Barber...113

The Healing Power of Music...114

Godmothers...116

Nostalgia...119

Two Brains ...121

Uncles...123

Disappointment...125

A Regular Cane...127

Loyalty...128

It Takes Two...129

The Surgeon's Recovery...130

Brownies...131

Getting Her Hard-Head Back...132

An Early Discharge...134

My Battle Scar...135
Friendship...136
Television...137
Love...138
Cradle Cap and Baby Oil...139
Digital Clocks...140
Index Cards...141
A Lesson From an Old Friend...142
"Cut Loose"...145
The Gift of Giving...146
Trust...148
Letting Go...149
A Six Month Pass...150
Staying Awake All Day...151
College Homecoming...152
Sharing Good Memories...154
Anger...155
A Time to Remain Silent...157
A Time to Speak...159
A Lap Desk...160
Kindergarten Books...161
A Good Gynecologic Exam...162
A Meaningful Thanksgiving...164
Wonder...167
Mama, I Remember Your Name...170
Reading, Writing, and Arithmetic...171
"Thank You" Christmas Cards...172
My Brain and My Heart: A Good Mix...174
Priceless Christmas Gifts...176
A Year of Miracles...179

Dedication

In the spirit of gratitude
To every person with the courage to persevere when quitting is easier,
to every person with the heart to give, expecting nothing in return,
may you continue to be rewarded with
earnest Hope
constant Faith
unwavering Strength
unconditional Love
infinite Wisdom
endless Joy

everlasting Peace.

Introduction

"Life is what happens while you are busy making other plans."
Allen Saunders

Life happens. Sometimes it rattles you to the core, leaving you questioning your own capabilities. Sometimes it temporarily knocks you off your feet and you bounce back, only to get knocked down again. At other times it can bring you to your knees, as it did to me in 1996 when an engagement abruptly ended, followed by the loss of a younger brother. When I got up off my knees, I got up journaling, specifically "gratitude journaling." It was journaling that helped me cope with the loss and made me a more grateful person, so I decided to make it a habit. It has guided me through every life-changing event since then and helped me avoid a few pitfalls. It also set me on the path of pursuing a lifelong dream to write.

In 2014, wanting to dig deeper into the true meaning of gratitude, I researched the word for the entire year and learned that it is so much more than a quick "thank you," or saying grace before meals, two things I was taught as a child. Gratitude is a state of being, and I wanted to develop a consciousness of gratitude. The more I learned, the better I felt; so in 2015 I decided to send gratitude messages to a handful of people each day. Each one of them found the messages encouraging, and by the end of the year, I had decided to turn those messages into a book. I didn't know what the book would look like, but I remembered some advice I received from Maya Angelou in 2004 while attending a conference where she was a keynote speaker: "if you want to be a good writer, keep writing." Hence I spent 2016 writing about gratitude and made plans to attend a writer's conference in February, 2017, to begin the next leg of my writing journey - publication. It would be a birthday present to myself. But life intruded again, and I had to put my plans on hold. This time I was shaken to the core by my daughter Mia's sudden illness.

Mia had been a vibrant thirty-seven-year old. She was a full-time nurse, part time student, and was known around town for her unique crochet designs. The crochet designs were a hobby that was evolving into a business that she loved as much as she loved taking care of sick babies and the elderly. Even though I thought she was overdoing it, she was doing what Mia wanted to do and for her that was all that mattered, until January 9, 2017, when she suffered a massive stroke that landed her in the hospital for fifty-two days.

Strokes aren't new to me, as you will learn later. Growing up in the sixties, I remember hearing the word, but it was always in a conversation about elderly people. What *is* new is the significant increase in the number of people under forty having strokes. Mia was in that category. According to the National Stroke Association, there was a 44 percent increase in the number of young Americans hospitalized due to stroke over the last decade. I'm a public health servant who has worked in health promotion for almost 30 years so I look at a lot of statistics. The stroke numbers were particularly alarming to me for two reasons: Mia had just been added to the statistic, and maybe there was something I could do to prevent other young people from being added to the number.

So you might ask, "What about a stroke is there to be grateful about?" After all, no one in their right mind would say "Thank you God for this stroke." Mia and I aren't saying that either. What we are saying is this: Mia had the stroke, and there was nothing we could do to reverse it. However, I decided early on that I would share our gratitude for the lessons and blessings we experienced along the way, hoping that sharing our story would be a blessing to others.

The Stroke That Touched My Heart is a tool that introduces the hidden gifts of practicing gratitude to anyone who has experienced a life-changing event, whether it is a medical diagnosis, a loss, trauma, or any personal crisis. You only need to look around you to witness the increasing number of young people struggling with life issues and turning to quick fixes such as drugs, alcohol, becoming slaves to digital technology, excessive shopping, violence, and other dangerous habits, only to find that they are spiraling out of control. They constantly search for happiness that always seems to be short-lived.

Gratitude is a practice that teaches you to appreciate what you already have and to realize that when you put things in proper perspective, what you have is enough. Adopting a consciousness of gratitude helps you connect with your inner power, and when you know your inner power, you no longer have to search for it in other people, places and things. Learning to be grateful ends the illusive search for peace and leads to a more meaningful life.

The Stroke That Touched My Heart chronicles how life unfolded for Mia and me from January 9, 2017 through January 9, 2018. At the end of each entry, we share our gratitude lesson. Then we ask you to take a few minutes to journal about your own experiences. Our story is a testament to the theory that we learn best by doing, and we feel that practicing gratitude will set you on the path to feeling more grateful. Even science has begun to recognize the overall health benefits of gratitude and how it increases healing. Of course we want you to read the book, but we also want you to invest the time in journaling in order to let go of the quick fixes that aren't working. When you work on gratitude, gratitude works on you: gradually, you begin to change on the inside, and when you change on the inside, your life changes.

Although all entries were written by me, some are Mia's words and some are mine. Where Mia's name appears, I did my best to say it the way she spoke at the time in order to give you a better picture of how the stroke affected the language center of her brain. Her speech was slow, sometimes with long pauses (as indicated by the "...."), as she struggled to think of the right words to say, and how to pronounce them. As she still reminds me two years later, "I know what I want to say, but the words just don't come out right." My reply is always the same, "I get what you're trying to say." We hope you will get it too. We also hope that something on these pages will inspire you to live a more grateful life, regardless of the circumstances.

DISCLAIMER: We are not spiritual or religious experts. These are our opinions based on our experiences.

January 9, 2017

Intuition

MYRTLE

Today began like most Mondays. I woke up around 4:30 a.m., sat up in bed, picked up my journal and pen and started writing, beginning with my gratitude list. This had been a practice for several years now, what I call my daily meditation. After finishing my gratitude list, I wrote to clear my head of anything that was bothering me and any adjustments I needed to make when it came to matters of the heart. Once I finished, I read one or two inspirational messages, and jotted down a few notes on what they meant to me and how I could use them to become a better person. Journaling always felt good, like praying on paper and leaving it there until the next time. I finished, got dressed, and headed to work.

I am the regional manager of the Health Promotion Division for the state of Tennessee. Our division is typically busy; today was no different. I enjoy my work most days and today I sailed through and left at 4:30 p.m. with yarn on my mind. I had a new crochet project I wanted to start, so I headed to the store to look for new yarn. I was low on gas, so I filled up my tank since there was a gas station right in front of the store. I pulled up to the pump, filled up the tank, and got back into the car. I started the ignition and slowly pulled away from the station, contemplating whether I really should buy more yarn. I had plenty at home, including some I had ordered and never taken out of the box. Mia and I often laughed about how we had become yarn junkies. We would see a pattern we liked and either order new yarn or run out and buy some, even though we knew that we could work on only one project at a time. We also knew that sometimes we already had the yarn we needed, so what sense did it make to keep buying more? None. But we kept buying it.

I was slowly driving toward the store, all the while in a serious debate with myself, so I pulled into a parking space. I sat there for a couple of minutes, thinking about the new pattern and trying to remember what yarn I had at home that would work for the project. I couldn't remember, so an inner voice said to me, "Go home and see what you have." I put the car in drive, pulled out of the parking lot and headed home.

I got there around 5:30, and Mia's car was in her parking space. That was odd since she was usually gone by this time; she had to be at work at 6:00 p.m. I didn't give it much thought; maybe today she was running a few minutes late or maybe she had switched shifts with a co-worker. I unlocked the door and immediately looked to the left toward her room. She was lying on the floor, on her back with her fan just a few feet away. The room was dark. Still not thinking much of it, I asked, "Girl what are you doing lying on that floor with that fan in your face? Do you know what time it is?" I expected her to burst out laughing at any minute and tell me that she was not going to work. But she didn't.

When she responded I could barely understand her. She was babbling, and her speech was slurred. Her left arm flailed as she struggled to speak. I moved closer. She didn't have on a top, only her shorts. Vomit was on the floor, on her chest, and in her hair. I smelled feces. Her left leg was bent at the knee, and it constantly moved back and forth. She pointed to her right side which was motionless, and she kept trying to speak, but the words were jumbled. At that point it hit me - my child has had a stroke. I felt sick to my stomach, like I wanted to vomit, but I told myself not to panic. I knew the first thing to do was to call 911.

OUR GRATITUDE LESSON: Divine intuition always has your best interest at heart. I'm most grateful I listened to my inner voice and came home.

YOUR GRATITUDE STORY: Intuition comes in many forms. It may be a feeling or a knowing that you can't ignore. It can be a dream or a physical sign. Describe a time when you followed your intuition and how it made you feel.

Emergency Medical Technicians (EMT)

I carry a small purse so under ordinary circumstances it wouldn't have been hard to find my cell phone, but this time I couldn't put my hands on it. "Don't panic" is what I kept repeating to myself. I knew that timing was critical. So I stopped, got down on my knees beside Mia, and asked God to please get us through this. I got up off my knees, went to my purse, reached in for the phone, found it, and called 911. I told the operator that my child had a stroke. She asked the routine questions, and I answered them as best I could. I ended the call and got back down on the floor.

Mia was still babbling and moving her left leg, trying her best to tell me what happened. That was good. At least she was still conscious, and I would do what I could to keep her that way until the paramedics arrived. I got up and went to the bathroom to get a towel to try to clean her up. Just inside the bathroom door, I noticed braids of hair on the floor and in the sink. She had obviously been cutting the extensions from her hair when the stroke began. That explained why her head looked different. She had removed about half of the extensions, which meant she had to have started much earlier in the day in order to be finished in enough time to get dressed for work.

I began thinking ahead. What about the medication that can reverse the effects of a stroke if it's administered within a certain timespan that the stroke occurs, somewhere between three to four hours if I remembered correctly? I thought about it as I grabbed a towel and went back to start cleaning her up. Vomit was matted in her hair, which made it almost impossible to clean. I wondered why she didn't have a top on and looked around the room to see where it was. I spotted it on the floor, picked it up, and slipped it on her. The answer as to why she didn't have it on came later.

She continued to babble and all I could say was, "hang in there, the ambulance is on the way." I felt helpless. Both of us just kept repeating ourselves and honestly, it was all we could do. Even though I had only been home for a few minutes, it felt like hours. I watched her and prayed and listened for a siren. "What was taking them so long?" I got up and went to the door, opened it, and looked out. Nothing. I called 911 again, and the operator assured me that the ambulance was in route. "But I don't hear any sirens and they should have been here by now," I insisted. "Ma'am," she replied in a calm tone, "It's only been four minutes since you first called and they are on their way. Just stay with your daughter and they will be there shortly." "But are you sure they have the right address?" I asked. She repeated the address I'd given her. It was correct. She gave the location of the drivers and said once again that they would be there momentarily.

I got back on the floor beside Mia, rubbing her forehead and face. Her skin felt cool and sweaty. Her left leg kept moving. She looked at me while pointing toward her bathroom, and it was obvious that she knew what she wanted to say, but again, all that came from her mouth were jumbled words.

Finally I heard sirens. I went to the door, looked out, and once I saw the ambulance rounding the corner, I walked outside and waved my hands. The driver noticed me and parked. He and an attendant got out and went to the back of the ambulance to get the stretcher. When they got to the door, I pointed them toward Mia lying on the floor. They looked at her and began asking routine questions, some of the same questions I had answered when I spoke to the operator. I really wanted them to get her up and out of there, but I understood the protocol.

They asked if I knew what time it all happened, a question that neither Mia nor I could answer. I knew where they were headed with the stroke medication and the window of time. All I could give them was the approximate time I found her. I thought about her cell phone and wondered if we could determine the time by looking at her call history. I figured that since she was conscious when I found her, maybe she had tried to call someone.

I began searching for her phone as they continued to assess her. I spotted it on the edge of her bed. Some of her bedcovers were on the bed, and some were on the floor. I would later learn that she had been trying to reach the phone herself but couldn't move so she had tried pulling the covers close to her, hoping that the phone would fall on the floor where she could reach it and call for help. Her efforts were fruitless.

For now, we needed to get into that phone so I grabbed it and started pushing the keys. After a few tries, I realized I needed a passcode to unlock it. The only person with the passcode was Mia and right now she couldn't even give the paramedics her name, let alone a passcode. This was confirmation that trying to reverse the effects of the stroke with the special medication was not going to be an option. Again, I felt nauseated, and I could feel my heart racing. I reminded myself to calm down and remain strong, both for myself and for Mia. We had to work with what we had; she was alive and fighting, and help had arrived.

After a few more questions, they put Mia on the stretcher and rolled her out to the ambulance, hooked her up to some equipment, and headed toward the hospital. I followed in my car, caution lights flashing. It seemed to me that the ambulance was creeping along. In hindsight, it was my mind racing. As I trailed them, I reminded myself that things could have been a lot worse. I felt grateful for the voice that said "go home" as I sat in the store parking lot. It was the voice I call intuition.

I was also grateful for a friendly pair of paramedics. From the call center staff to the paramedics and ambulance drivers, EMTs rarely get the recognition they deserve. Most of us don't think about them until we hear blaring sirens, and even then, our thoughts are not thoughts of gratitude, they are demanding thoughts. EMTs brave every kind of weather and may walk into horrific environments, sometimes saving lives, sometimes not. So the next time you spot those red lights flashing and have to pull over to allow an ambulance to pass, or you are awakened by a screaming siren in the early morning hours, remember to be grateful for the risks they take and the services they provide.

OUR GRATITUDE LESSON: The future has a sneaky way of arriving unrehearsed and when it does, there are always people who are prepared to step in and help us get through it. Honor them.

YOUR GRATITUDE STORY: List five reasons to be grateful for EMTs.

Emergency Rooms (ER)

Finally we arrived at the ER. When the EMTs opened the ambulance door to roll Mia out, I was happy to see that her left leg was propped up, and moving back and forth, which for me meant she was still fighting. I desperately wanted to follow the paramedics into the ER. I knew I would be stopped, so I parked my car in the lot designated for families. I knew the layout of the ER well enough to find my way to the waiting area. Once I got there, I knew I had to check in, get a green sticker and wait for Mia to be triaged and assigned to a room.

Once I checked in, I was told that Mia was being triaged, which was both good and bad news. It was good news that she was being evaluated quickly and not just parked in a corner, but a part of me felt that things would be better if I were in the room with her to answer questions and observe. I knew that Mia couldn't answer, and incorrect information could sometimes be the difference between life and death. But I couldn't get into the room.

I asked the receptionist if she knew how long it would be before Mia would be checked in, and of course I received the answer that everyone gets: "We will let you know as soon as we hear something ma'am." I couldn't sit still, and so I walked around the area, hoping to get a glance of Mia, the paramedics, or perhaps my niece, who was an ER nurse. However, I didn't see anyone I recognized, so I just had to wait it out. Waiting was hard, but feeling helpless while waiting was even harder.

Dealing with stroke patients was not new to me. Mia's dad had had a stroke at the age of 33; a stroke that resulted from blunt force trauma on the job and left him partially paralyzed on his right side. We were living in New York at the time. I will never forget that night. I was in nursing school and in the middle of a divorce. I heard about the accident through a friend and decided to stop by the hospital to check on him. While standing at his bedside, I heard this gurgling sound in his throat and remembered from one of my classes that the sound was not good for a stroke patient, so I alerted the nurse in charge. She came to the room and evaluated him and then quickly notified the doctor. The gurgling sound was the sound of blood flowing from an artery in his brain that had burst, which meant he was literally drowning in his own blood. He was transferred to a trauma hospital in the Bronx, where emergency surgery saved his life.

Fast forward thirty plus years, and here I was in the hospital ER with our 37-year-old daughter, wondering if there was a connection, and if so, what it was? Questions from the past started running through my head, and taking up too much space, so I reminded myself to stay in the present. I got that message loud and clear when I found Mia on the floor: "now" is all we have. So I would do what I'd always done when there was a family crisis; I would put my emotions aside and follow logic. It was the only way I knew to cope. I come from a large family which meant there always seemed to be some type of crisis happening. If I went with my emotions, I would have crumbled long time ago. No, I needed to stay focused for Mia and for my own well-being.

Since I had time on my hands, I needed to notify our family, but my phone wouldn't pick up a signal in that particular part of the ER. I was not about to walk outside and risk missing hearing my name called when it was time to go back to be with Mia, so I waited and thought about who to call first. It wasn't long before I heard my name called. I anxiously made my way to the counter, got my green permission sticker, and was taken back to Mia's room.

The ER staff was busy doing what they routinely do, and I was relieved to see Mia with that left leg still bent and moving. We made eye contact and her eyes told me how glad she was that I was finally with her. I stood beside her, rubbing her head, hoping to put some of her fears to rest, and assuring her that everything would be all right.

I took a seat while staff came in and out to draw blood, run tests, and check monitors. As I sat, I dreaded having to contact family. For one thing, I hated being the bearer of bad news. Secondly, I didn't want to keep repeating such a heart-ripping, gut-wrenching story. But, I had no choice, I had to do it.

I started with my son Cameron who lived in Chattanooga. I knew this would be hard for him to accept and I really wished I could have been there to tell him in person, but I couldn't so I did the best I could on the phone. When I told him that Mia had had a stroke, there was complete silence. I knew he was struggling with processing what he had heard. I didn't want to break down, so I kept quiet for what seemed like a long time, waiting for him to speak. When he did, there was a faint tremble in his voice. I knew he was fighting back tears. So was I. Nonetheless, the logical side of me said to him in as calm a voice as I could, "Listen, faith and prayer will get us through this crisis just as it has gotten us through others." I let him know that Mia was awake and as alert as she could be, given the circumstances. I asked him to hold on to the one thing he knew to be true about his sister: she was a fighter. That seemed to put him somewhat at ease. I asked him to call their brother Warren, and to stay put for now. I promised I would update him as soon as I spoke to a doctor. With trepidation, he said "okay."

Next, I needed to contact my brothers, so I started with my brother Bill and asked him to get word to the other siblings. I then called Raymond, a brother with a different mother and asked him to get word to his siblings. I don't remember who was next, but the news traveled fast, as bad news usually does, and it wasn't long before my phone was constantly ringing and crowded with messages. By that time it was getting late, and I didn't have the energy to keep repeating myself. Logic kicked in, and I cut the phone off. Immediate family had been notified and I needed to pay close attention to what was going on in front of me: Mia.

Before long Bill showed up. Mia recognized him when he walked through the glass doors of the ER holding room. Right away she started trying to tell to him what happened, but her speech wasn't any better than it had been hours earlier, so she became a bit agitated. He told her to calm down, looked at me, and said, "She's still being Mia," suggesting that she was still hard-headed. He knew her well. "Yep," I replied, "and this time, being hard-headed is a good thing."

As we sat there waiting for the doctor to come in with test results, Bill's phone rang and it was Cameron. I knew he would call Bill since the two of them were pretty close. Bill said to him: "This is your dad all over again." It was interesting that I wasn't the only one experiencing *déjà vu*.

After a few minutes, the ER started to get to Bill. I noticed him wiping sweat from his forehead, and I found a washcloth and handed it to him, asking if he was okay. He said he just needed to step outside to get some air. He made it just outside the door and stopped, leaning against the glass wall. I walked out and asked if I needed to get staff to help him. Again he said no, but I could see that he was sweating even more.

He had never done well when it came to sickness or death. I remembered years back when our younger brother Calvin was dying. We were at Mama's and a few family members had come to be with us. As we all sat in Calvin's room talking, Calvin had a seizure. His body stiffened and he began to shake and jerk violently. His eyes rolled back in his head his arms were flailing. Bill, who was sitting in a rocking chair right beside the bed jumped up and ran out the room, leaving the rocker moving back and forth as if it was battery operated. That was over 20 years ago, and we still laughed about it. But this was no laughing matter. I knew Bill was getting nervous, so I told him to go home, that I would keep him posted. I couldn't handle two patients right now.

The night was long. Unknowingly, it was a prelude to the days ahead. After a battery of tests confirmed the stroke, sometime during the early morning hours Mia was transferred to the neurology floor. Her blood pressure was normal. Her cholesterol levels were within normal range. She was not diabetic and had no history of heart disease. Although in 2008 she had been diagnosed with lupus, she had not experienced a lupus crisis, or at least she had not mentioned it to me or shown any visible signs. So I was back to the initial question: What caused the stroke?

I didn't have the answer. All I had were speculations, which weren't helpful at all. It was time to let go and focus on what I did have. I had Mia, who had hung on to life from the time the stroke attacked her brain until the time I found her. I had family and a good support system. We lived in a city with a good hospital less than 15 minutes away, which meant no out of town travel. I had faith. Yes, I had enough to be thankful for.

OUR GRATITUDE LESSON: An emergency room is a good reminder to give up the delusion that you're always in control of the situation. Sometimes no matter how much you want to be in control, you are not. I surrendered and did my best to control what I could control, which was my thinking.

YOUR GRATITUDE STORY: List five things that emergency room personnel do that you can't do.

January 10

Prayer

 Myrtle

The neurology staff was constantly in and out of the room, drawing blood, resetting beeping pumps, checking vitals and monitoring neurologic functioning. Mia was starting to complain of a headache. Although her speech was slurred, she pointed to her head and communicated well enough to let us know that she was in pain. The doctor had ordered something for pain, but it wasn't working. Despite the pain, she still kept that left leg bent and in constant motion. I continued to connect it to her determination not to give up. I felt that she believed that if she could keep that leg moving until I got home from work, she would survive. I would learn months later that my assumption was correct.

I stayed at her bedside, hoping to see signs of improvement and waiting for a doctor to show up with some answers. She'd had none of the classic symptoms of a stroke. She and I had often joked about her cholesterol and blood pressure levels always being normal, despite what she ate. We had even started a little competition to see whose readings would be the lowest when we got our checkups. Her levels were always lower than mine and I was on blood pressure medication. So I was stumped. The only probable cause I could come up with was stress.

I asked the nurse for the name of the neurologist who would be treating Mia, and what time he usually made his rounds. She told me he made his rounds around 8:00 a.m. Even though deep down within I knew he would not bring the news that I desperately wanted to hear, his reassurance that she would get better would suffice for now.

I knew this would be a long journey, and it came to me while sitting there waiting that the only way to get through it without it negatively affecting my health, would be to journal my way through it. I had withstood some tough times thanks to journaling, so I knew what I needed to do once I talked to the doctor - I had to go home and get my survival kit, my prayer kit, which consisted of my journal, a pen, and my daily inspirational reading. My faith was strong, and journaling would help me cope with my feelings as well as with my fears. I knew Mia was a fighter. I believed that we were going to be okay.

Between 8:00 and 9:00 a.m. the neurologist knocked on the door of Mia's room, came in, shook my hand, and introduced himself. He told me what I already knew - that Mia had had a very serious stroke caused by what is called a carotid dissection. He explained that a dissection occurs when the carotid artery in the neck ruptures and blood spills over into the brain, causing other complications and resulting in a stroke. He said that sometimes the dissection causes death and sometimes it doesn't. As he was explaining all of this, Mia was lying there quietly watching me. I think she was trying her best to see how I was reacting to what the doctor was saying. I couldn't let her see me rattled.

I asked the doctor what caused the artery in her neck to break, since she had none of the classic symptoms of a stroke. He answered with a question of his own: "Has she had any recent falls or been involved in an accident that could have caused trauma to her head?" "Not that I'm aware of," I answered. He then said something along the lines of... there are sometimes just freak acts of nature that can't be explained, and this could be one of them. What he said didn't make sense to me, or maybe it just wasn't what I wanted to hear. He also mentioned that his clinic had seen an increase in the number of young people having strokes, and they were not sure why. He assured me that the staff would be taking good care of Mia, and that he was going to get her into rehab as quickly as possible.

When the doctor left, I sat down to try and process what I'd heard. To be honest, his answers left me with more questions than I'd had before he walked into the room. Nonetheless, at this point I knew I had to be grateful that Mia would immediately begin rehab and that would put her on the road to recovery. I knew I couldn't get caught up in worrying about unanswered questions. I'd experienced enough challenges to know that worry was a thief that would suck the life out of me if I let it. I would not. I had to help Mia get back on her feet. I thanked God that things were looking as positive as they were, then got up and found the nurse and told her that I had to leave for a few minutes. It was time to run home to get my prayer kit. I knew that prayer was more than words uttered from desperate hearts. For me, prayer had become a way to heighten my awareness of the presence of God, and this situation was an opportunity to test not only my faith, but my practice. Yes, my first journal entry for the day would be thanking God in advance that everything would work out for the best.

OUR GRATITUDE LESSON: If you are praying, why worry? If you are worrying, why pray? There is no need to do both.

YOUR GRATITUDE STORY: What worries you most? Try this worry game: Buy yourself a good sized jar and create a "worry jar." Keep your jar in in a private place where you won't see it, sort of your own secret closet. Each time something begins to bother you, grab a piece of paper, write it down, fold it, and put it in the jar and leave it there. Say to yourself, "I'm leaving this worry to a higher power." Then move on with your day. Keep doing it every time a new worry comes about. After a period of time, say six months to a year, see how many prayers were answered, how many worries were forgotten. You will also discover that about half of what you worried about never happened, so why allow it to steal your joy?

January 11

Hope

 MYRTLE

It is day two in the hospital, and Mia is awake and responsive. Her speech is still slurred, she's frustrated, and her headaches are not letting up. Calls, visits, and prayers are coming from family, friends, and co-workers. I got an early morning text from a friend that put things in perspective for the day. It read: "No matter who we are or what our challenge is in life, there is always a 'nevertheless'- some positive thing we can look at or talk about that brings the rest of life into perspective. So the next time you are tempted to complain about your life in any way, go ahead and state your complaint, and then say, 'nevertheless,' and find something positive about your life to offset the complaint." Mercy! I pulled out my journal, read the text again and wrote: Mia had suffered a massive stroke - nevertheless, she was still here and still fighting for her life, and for now, that was enough.

OUR GRATITUDE LESSON: Hope is pairing prayer with thanksgiving and believing in the impossible.

YOUR GRATITUDE STORY: List one thing you hope for and describe what you are doing to keep that hope from dying.

January 12

Diagnostic Tests

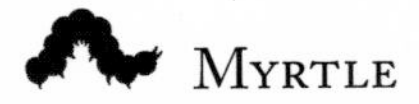 MYRTLE

Day three and the neurologist and primary care doctor make their rounds, and still there are no answers to what caused the stroke. Neither of them seemed to think it was connected to Mia's lupus, but they weren't sure. They had run several tests. The neurologist asked me if there was any history of heart disease in the family, and I answered "yes," so he ordered a battery of heart tests. He wanted to be sure they hadn't missed something. The tests came back normal, therefore the treatment plan was to give Mia intense speech, occupational, and physical therapy. When the doctors left, I went around to the left side of Mia's bed to ask her if she understood what the doctors had said. She looked at me and gave me a "thumbs up." I forced myself to give her a smile.

I'm grateful to be living in a country whose healthcare system ranks among the best in the world when it comes to diagnostic testing and identifying problems. It's a service we rarely think about until we need it, and even then, we think of it as an entitlement rather than a service. I thought about how things would have been if we had lived in an underdeveloped country.

OUR GRATITUDE LESSON: Be grateful for inventors, inventions, and the services they bring. Every need brings what is needed.

YOUR GRATITUDE STORY: Look around your home. What are five inventions that you wouldn't want to live without?

January 13

A Craniectomy

 MYRTLE

Around 9:00 a.m., I noticed that Mia was not as alert as she had been. When I asked her a question, she would open her mouth but not even a slurred word came out. I opened her eyes and noticed that her pupils were dilated. That was not a good sign, so I found the nurse and asked her to come and take a look. She assessed Mia and agreed that her neurologic status was changing. She immediately contacted the neurologist. Within a matter of minutes he came up to evaluate Mia and ordered an MRI. I knew it was serious. Just a few minutes later she was taken downstairs for the test. I was told that she would be there for about an hour, and I should wait in her room for a call from the doctor. It would be another long wait.

I could not sit still and was standing at the nurses' station when the phone rang. Mia's nurse answered, and I could tell from her facial and verbal expressions that the news was not good. She handed me the phone. The neurologist informed me that pressure from the stroke had begun to build up and was affecting the right side of Mia's brain, which explained why she was not as alert, and why she was drifting off and unable to speak. He went on to say that if the pressure was not released, it would lead to paralysis of the left side of her body and the brain compression would ultimately shut all her vital organs down. He recommended surgery immediately, a craniectomy; however he told me that the decision was mine to make. He told me that if I chose surgery, he would have a neurosurgeon come up to explain the procedure and get her in the operating room right away: the sooner, the better. Since doing nothing was not an option, I gave him a nod to go ahead and contact the surgeon. I waited. In the meantime, the transporters brought Mia back to the room. She was even less responsive than she had been before she went down for the MRI. Her left leg, the gauge I used to indicate that she was still fighting, was motionless. My armpits started to itch; my palms got sweaty. All I could do was pray, and my prayer included thanking God in advance for a successful craniectomy.

Craniectomies weren't new to me either. Thirty plus years ago my nursing class had observed brain surgery to remove tumors from a patient's brain. There was nothing ordinary about watching the surgeon drill into the patient's skull as tiny pieces flew into his goggles while a nurse used gauze to remove sweat from his brow. The surgery took hours, since there were multiple tumors to be removed. As we students left the observation deck, the surgeon was visibly agitated, the nurses appeared to be pressured, and that operating room was not a pretty sight. Hopefully things had advanced in the OR since then.

In just a few minutes the neurosurgeon arrived to explain the craniectomy. He didn't speak in long complicated words and phrases the way some doctors do. I sensed that he was a kind-spirited gentleman who cared about his patients, and that he had years of experience. He took his time and described the procedure, which he referred to as a "piece of cake." He would remove a piece of her skull, about the size of a fist, in order for the brain to have some room to swell on the outside instead of swelling within and shutting her body down. He explained that the piece of skull that he removed would be kept in a sterile solution in a special place in the hospital until it was time to replace it, which would be several weeks down the road. With my consent, he would immediately get things rolling, beginning with sending an anesthesiologist to assess Mia. I nodded my consent. All the while, Mia was lying there motionless.

When he left the room, I contacted the family. A few minutes later the anesthesiologist came up to ask a few questions and explain his role in the surgery. Shortly after he left, Mia was taken down for surgery, and I was told to wait in her room. By that time my brother Dwight, a niece, and two cousins had come to be stay with me. It felt good to have them there. Their presence kept me from having flashbacks of the surgery I had observed some 30 years ago.

OUR GRATITUDE LESSON: Thank God for medical advances. The first craniectomy was performed on the patient while he was awake. Imagine that!

YOUR GRATITUDE STORY: What medical invention(s) have you or a loved one had to use and how has it made your life better?

A Neurosurgeon's "Piece of Cake"

 Myrtle

It was early afternoon when the surgeon called to tell me that everything went well, as he expected. Being the trooper that she is, Mia had gone through the surgery without mishap and was doing well. She was in recovery and from there would be taken to the Intensive Care Unit (ICU) to be closely monitored. He explained that he didn't expect any complications, but it was protocol for anyone who went through a craniectomy to go to the ICU. He also assured me that she would soon begin to show signs of improvement. I thanked him and hung up the phone, relieved and ready to get to the ICU.

Mia's brothers arrived later that evening. Cameron hadn't been in an ICU before and I knew that hospitals made him extremely uncomfortable, so I did my best to prepare them all for the visit. I let them know some of what to expect: monitors, catheters, IVs, a central line in her neck, drainage bags, tubes, pumps, beeps, and alarms. I told them that Mia would be connected to one of the most critical and intimidating pieces of equipment in the ICU, the ventilator, which was literally breathing for her until her lungs could resume breathing on their own. I warned them that they would see a tube in her mouth that connected her to the ventilator and that she was heavily sedated, which is often required when the tube is inserted. She would be drowsy and unable to talk, even though she would want to say something. I explained that since all patients were frightened when they woke up in the ICU, Mia would have restraints on her wrists and would want us to remove them, so we would have to reassure her that they were there for a reason. I warned them that because of the pressure that had built up in her brain, her face and head would be swollen, but not to be too alarmed. Last, I asked them to be strong for their sister so that we didn't add to her fears. Their facial expressions told me that all this would be a lot easier for Warren to grasp than Cameron, but that their presence would help Mia and it had to be done.

We entered the ICU together; I held Cameron's hand and Warren's wife held his. Mia's eyes were open. She recognized us and extended her restrained left hand to touch ours. Hugging was impossible and really not the healthiest thing to do, so one at a time we quietly honored her non-verbal cues by squeezing her hand. I knew she wanted to know what had happened to her, so I did my best to explain the surgery and why she was in ICU. I told her that if she continued to do well, the endotracheal tube would soon be taken out of her mouth, enabling her to speak and possibly leave the unit in a day or two. She squeezed my hand to let me know she understood. We explained to her that we were not going to stay too long because she needed to rest, but that we would be in the hospital around the clock and would come back to check on her throughout the night.

I've often heard people say they wouldn't want to be placed on life support to be kept alive; that when it's their time to go, they want to go. It's not for me to question anyone's beliefs when it comes to making medical decisions such as the one I had to make for Mia; every person and every situation is different. I had to follow my beliefs that God worked through people and that things would play out for Mia's good. I trusted that the skilled, steady hands of the neurosurgeon would do what he promised to do. He did. I believed that Mia would come through the surgery just fine. She did.

Not only are we grateful to the neurosurgeon and the neurologist, but to all neurosurgeons who make a living performing craniectomies, craniotomies, and brain surgery. From Hippocrates' 5th century B.C. teachings on the subject to the 20th century when the new and autonomous discipline of neurosurgery began to evolve, these men and women have made a huge difference. For the person in distress they offer hope, and in many cases they restore life, one surgery at a time. Mia's doctor described her craniectomy as "a piece of cake," which for me and most others is hard to fathom. But if you compare it to the first craniectomies performed around 8000 to 5000 B.C., without anesthesia, I guess it makes the term "a piece of cake" easier to digest. It's been said that what you do is not work, unless you would rather be doing something else.

OUR GRATITUDE LESSON: "Let us rise up and be thankful, for if we didn't learn a lot today, at least we learned a little, and if we didn't learn a little, at least we didn't get sick, and if we got sick, at least we didn't die; so, let us all be thankful." -Buddha

YOUR GRATITUDE STORY: List five things you love about being alive.

January 14

Joy

 Myrtle

On day two in the ICU Mia began breathing on her own so the pulmonologist took her off the ventilator. She was well on her way to being discharged and going back to the neurology floor. There was a steady flow of family and friends, so many that I decided to greet them in the hospital's cafeteria. They brought food, cards, gift baskets, words of comfort, and even laughter. For the first time since January 9, I felt joy. I could say with conviction that even in what could seemingly be the worst situation, one can experience joy.

I felt it when Mia's hand touched mine in the ICU. I felt it as family and friends showed up at a time when I didn't want to be alone. I began to understand that I didn't have to do anything to feel joy. The pain had run so deep that it somehow removed all barriers and opened me up to an inner knowledge that everything would be alright.

Warren and his wife wanted to spend the night at the hospital and suggested that I go home and get some rest. I took them up on their offer and for the first time in six days, I went home and slept in my own bed. It felt good and peaceful, like it was the right place to be, despite the circumstances.

I woke up early the next morning and began journaling. I had a long list of things to be thankful for, beginning with Mia, family, friends, the surgeon, and the ICU. I wrote about life's ebbs and flows and how in some ways life is similar to the seasons and in some ways it isn't. The seasons change around the same time each year, and while we would like to think that life's changes are as predictable, they are not. The best laid plans can be interrupted without advance notice. It was winter, a season marked by frigid temperatures, long dark nights, and a natural slowing down of things. Despite Mia's best efforts, it had dealt her a cold blow, bringing all her activities to an abrupt halt. At the same time, the unyielding dark climate had forced me to look in a different direction, to stare pain in the face, and beg for mercy. However on the fifth day, joy sneaked in and brought with it a ray of sunshine that warmed my heart and taught me two life-changing lessons.

OUR GRATITUDE LESSON: Sorrow comes to us all. The deeper the sorrow, the more joy it can contain if you look for it.

YOUR GRATITUDE STORY: Joy is an inside job. Journal about at least one thing that ignites the joy inside you.

January 15

Good Luck Charms

 MYRTLE

Since she continued to show signs of improvement, Mia was discharged from the ICU and sent back to the neurology floor to resume her treatment plan. She needed lots of rest, so once again I had to find a place to receive the welcome flow of family and friends. This time I chose the neurology waiting area.

Cousin Sandra brought balloons with a little beige teddy bear attached. It was cute and caught Mia's attention. She motioned for me to add it to the others on the shelf, which was so full that I had to do some rearranging. After Sandra left, Mia looked at the shelf, pointing to the bear, smiling and nodding her head. She still wasn't able to say what she wanted to say. When she spoke, the words didn't flow the way she wanted them to and that only added to her frustration. It was hard for me not to interrupt her or try to finish her sentences, but I knew that for now, the best way to communicate with her was to ask simple questions that she could answer with a nod, a simple "yes" or "no," or sometimes a "thumbs up." I knew this new way of communicating would last for a while, but I believed that one day at a time, her speech would improve.

It took me a minute, but I finally understood why she kept looking at the bear on the shelf and smiling. She wanted me to cut it off the string and give it to her so she could put it in her bed. I didn't think much about it at the time; however a few days later she asked me about her dad's middle name. I told her that Thomas was actually his middle name and that his first name was Marion, a name he never used. So she decided to name the bear Marion and vowed that he was going to help her to get better. "Marion… you know… help me…with…" she said, pointing to her right side. I knew exactly what she meant. "He will bring you good"…I said, leaving her to fill in the blank. "Luck," she blurted out with a grin. "Yes…. and…. daddy…. too," she added.

From that day forward, Marion never left her side. She took him to every speech, occupational, and physical therapy session. If she went downstairs to the cafeteria, Marion went with her. If she forgot him, she would have staff or whoever was with her go back and get him. He was small enough to fit into the shirt pocket of the scrubs she wore every day, so all the rehab staff knew him and expected him to be in her pocket whenever she was outside her room. They treated Marion with as much respect as she did.

When she was in the room sitting in her wheelchair, Marion was in her pocket. If she was in bed, he was usually on the pillow or somewhere under the covers. Sometimes he ended up on the floor or shuffled around as she tossed and turned in her bed. When he did, in a panicky voice she would yell, "Where's....Marion?" I would remind her to turn her head to her right to find him. The stroke had left her partially blind in her right eye, so she had to turn her head in order to see things on her right, something she had not gotten used to doing. When she did, Marion was usually there. If he ended up on the floor, she would ask whoever was in the room to pick him up. Sometimes when only the two of us were in the room, she would gently scold Marion for not staying put, as if it was his fault that she accidently knocked him around, or out of the bed.

Other than my occasionally picking up a penny as a sign of good luck when we were together, Mia and I had never talked about good luck charms, and I wasn't about to initiate the conversation now. I did, however, give the matter some thought. To be honest, I believe we all have our good luck charms whether we want to admit it or not. We're all a little bit superstitious. We've crossed our fingers for good luck, put a rabbit's foot in our pockets, searched for a four-leaf clover, tossed a coin into a wishing well, or made a wish while blowing out candles on a birthday cake. We've knocked on wood as an expression of gratitude when something bad didn't happen to us. We've bought angels to symbolize protection. Call them silly or nonsense, but good luck charms are a part of many cultures. They are used in hospitals, at sporting events, and in religious settings, just to mention a few. Theoretically, they boost confidence and expectations, which can subsequently change the outcome of a situation. Mia believed in Marion and that was all that mattered.

OUR GRATITUDE LESSON: The people we recognize as superheroes are superheroes because they had supernatural beliefs.

YOUR GRATITUDE STORY: What good luck charms do you use?

January 16

Insurance

 Myrtle

Right after starting her new job Mia mentioned getting short-term disability insurance. She thought it was a good thing to do since she had lupus. I didn't know if she actually went through with her plans, so I contacted her employer and was told that she had purchased the insurance and what paperwork I would need to complete in order for her to begin receiving benefits. They would email the forms to me, and I needed to complete and return them as soon as possible in order to get the benefits started. Her benefits would last for only twelve weeks, but twelve were better than zero. The checks would help with some of her bills. Since she would not be returning to work anytime soon, her coverage would end after twelve weeks. In my mind, something else would fall into place, if I kept searching.

OUR GRATITUDE LESSON: Guarantees only last until the next one. Appreciate them while they last.

YOUR GRATITUDE STORY: List five guarantees you have in life, things you know for sure.

January 17

Helmets

MYRTLE

Mia started physical, speech, and occupational therapy today. Because of the craniectomy, the rehab doctor had ordered that she wear a customized protective helmet every minute that she was out of bed. Even though they serve a good purpose, almost no one likes to wear a helmet. To make matters worse, Mia's helmet didn't fit well. It was too big because the measurements had been taken before the surgery, before all her hair had been shaved from the left side of her head. She hated the way it looked, so she came up with a strategy. She would get every visitor to sign it so that the signatures covered what she called the "boring" color and embarrassing shape. Between the visitors and hospital staff, it took only a few days to cover every inch of the helmet. While she got quite a few unwanted stares, comments from observers always made her smile. Her strategy had worked; she turned an "ugly, boring" helmet into a positive conversation piece.

Without a protective helmet, a simple bump on the head could cause serious problems, and that was the last thing we wanted. It took a few days to remember to strap the helmet on before she stood up, especially when she got up in the middle of the night to go to the bathroom. Inevitably, one night she did slip and fall, and it was the only reminder she needed to be grateful for the helmet. After the fall, wearing it soon became second nature.

OUR GRATITUDE LESSON: Little nuggets are sometimes found in the most unlikely places. Treasure them all.

YOUR GRATITUDE STORY: Finish this sentence: One little thing that has made a big difference in my life____

January 18

Encouraging Words

 MYRTLE

Mia had two surprise visits today. One of her favorite grade school teachers and her teacher's aunt came to visit. The teacher had heard about Mia's stroke and stopped in to give her some encouraging words since she, too, had had a stroke and had made a remarkable recovery. She was there to show Mia that things would get better if she was willing to do the work. Mia hadn't seen this teacher in years, but her warm smile let her teacher know that she recognized her. Mia was quiet and very attentive as her teacher shared her experience, and just before leaving, she reminded Mia to give rehab a hundred percent effort. Mia gave her thumbs up and another reassuring smile.

The next visitor was one of Cameron's high school classmates. Mia's facial expression showed that she was "shocked" to see him. Afterall, he was not her friend, he was her brother's. He came into the room, gave me a hug, took a seat, and started talking. This young man was a comedian at heart. All anyone needed was a couple of minutes in his company, and they were guaranteed to laugh. We laughed, and it felt good. Even though Mia told me several days later that at first she was afraid to laugh because she thought it would make her head hurt more, she said she couldn't resist. "My head..." she said, pointing to her bandage, "didn't... hurt." That's because he and the teacher were God sent, I thought to myself.

OUR GRATITUDE LESSON: Words mean more than what is set down on paper. It takes the human voice to infuse them with deeper meaning. -Maya Angelou

YOUR GRATITUDE STORY: Who is the last person that delivered encouraging words to you? Did you thank her/him?

January 19

The World Wide Web

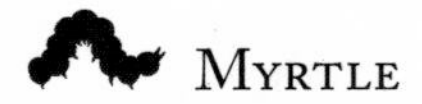

Myrtle

Mia had begun intensive rehab, so it was time for me to start making important decisions that she wasn't able to make for herself. The words "Power of Attorney" (POA) were buzz words that I'd heard in every business conversation I'd had regarding Mia. The bank, employers, insurers, hospital, Internal Revenue Service, debtors, doctors, all asked the same question: "Do you have Power of Attorney?" Each time my answer was "No." This was new to me, but I knew I had to move quickly, since "no" was not going to be an acceptable answer much longer.

I went on the Internet to do some research and learned that there were different types of POAs. I needed to be careful to choose the right one, so I consulted with an attorney, a friend of the family, to be sure I was on the right track. She assured me that I was and advised me what to do next. Bill downloaded the right forms for me, and my niece came to the hospital to notarize them. Now I could scratch that task off my list and move on to the next one.

Later that night, I thought about how things might have played out had I not had access to the web. It could have been quite costly in terms of time and money. I had the Internet, the computer, the attorney, my brother, and my niece to add to my gratitude list. I also thought about the people who use the Internet daily, the social media in particular, and never think to use it in situations such as this. I remembered something my son said to me a few years back: "Ma," he said matter-of-factly, "with the Internet and Google, the words 'I don't know' should never come out of anybody's mouth." It was something to consider.

OUR GRATITUDE LESSON: The information highway is as close as your fingertips and it can take you as far as you want to travel. Let it be your useful servant.

YOUR GRATITUDE STORY: List five ways you benefit from using the Internet.

January 22

Classmates

Myrtle

Two of Mia's classmates visited today. They brought her a beautiful plant, a card, money, and an angel, on behalf of the class of '97.' She didn't talk much, but sort of thanked them with her eyes and her smile. Days later after her speech improved, she told me how good it felt to know that they were thinking about her twenty years after graduation, and that the two people who visited were not classmates that she ran around with in school. I told her that obviously it didn't matter; they were thoughtful people.

GRATITUDE LESSON: Some memories are never forgotten. Instead they lie dormant until awakened by special moments when gifts of love can once again be shared. Cherish them.

YOUR GRATITUDE STORY: Think of five things you can do to cheer someone else up. Do one each week for five weeks and see how good it makes you feel.

January 24

Vigilance

 MYRTLE

Today marked Mia's fifteenth day in the hospital and I thought of three reasons to be grateful to have been able to be at her bedside each day. First I believed that being at her bedside on January 13 saved her life. She had good nurses who did the best they could, but they had way too many patients to give her the level of care she needed. My presence made a difference.

Second, I was grateful to have been in her room this morning when the occupational therapist came in. Before getting started Mia had to use the bathroom, so he offered to help get her on the bedside commode. We got her up, but it turned out to be a false alarm, however when we got her up from the commode, there was blood in the pan. The therapist looked at it, looked at me, and left the room. A few minutes later he returned with the floor and charge nurses, who both had questionable looks on their faces. The charge nurse looked at me and asked how long Mia had been bleeding. I told her that it had just started, and I was pretty sure it was blood from her menstrual cycle. "Oh, he had us a little concerned," she said, looking at the therapist. Umph," was all I could say. If he had only said something to me before he left the room, I would have told him that it was from her cycle. I could only wonder what might have happened if I had not been in the room. Would tests have been ordered? Would they have asked Mia, who wouldn't have been able to answer their questions or tell them anything about her cycle? Or would someone have just figured it out? I'll never know but I do know that once again, my presence made a difference.

The next day one of my nieces and her mother, who were both nurses, came to visit. The first thing they told me to do was to leave. "Run errands or just take some time for yourself," my sister-in-law commanded me. They were going to give Mia a bath, change her bed, and do what good nurses do. I trusted them and left. When I returned, Mia's skin was glowing, and the room smelled fresh and clean. Her smile said it all; their TLC had done her good.

Later in the afternoon, two physical therapists came to get Mia up and see how much movement she could tolerate. They introduced themselves, gave her a quick assessment, and started to get her up when one of them looked at the other and said: "Her skin looks a little flush, do you think we need to let the nurse know?" I looked at them and explained that her skin looked that way because she'd just had a bath and some good moisturizer applied to her skin, and it was glowing, not flushed. I assured them that there was nothing wrong. Both of them were young white women who obviously didn't know much about black folks' skin. They thanked me. This was the third reason I was glad to be at Mia's bedside. Again, I wondered how the day might have gone had I not been there.

OUR GRATITUDE LESSON: Give thanks for the "third eye" that helps you see what needs to be seen and the courage to do what needs to be done.

YOUR GRATITUDE STORY: List five things you like most about yourself. How do you use them to help others?

January 25

A Time To Search

 MYRTLE

Progress is slow and the days are long, leaving plenty of time for questions without answers. Questions like, when would I go back to work? Was it time for me to retire? Could we live decently on a reduced income? What about Mia's bills? What about the passwords to her accounts, passwords that I didn't know and she couldn't remember? When would I go to the Social Security Administration to apply for Mia's disability? Could the stroke have been avoided? Why couldn't I fix her medical condition? Had we lost the old Mia? What would the new Mia be like?

I've always asked questions. When I was growing up, my mother often warned me that I asked too many and that questioning grown folks was going to get me into trouble. And it did. But these were questions of a different type. They were tough questions, the kind that didn't have quick, easy answers, and that left me feeling alone and confused. As I sat there pondering, bottled-up tears streamed almost uncontrollably down my face, forcing me to turn my back to Mia so she didn't see me crying. They must have been cleansing tears because once they stopped, I felt better. I then pulled out my journal, wrote down every question that occupied way too much space in my head, and trusted that time would bring answers.

OUR GRATITUDE LESSON: Hidden in every cloud is a rainbow. Be grateful in advance for the wisdom to recognize it.

YOUR GRATITUDE STORY: What do you do when you have questions you can't answer? Here's a suggestion: Put them in your "worry jar." If they keep popping into your head, keep writing them down. The answers will come but you have to be paying attention to recognize them.

January 26

Home Remedies

 Myrtle

Mia's constant headaches meant she had to take opioids around the clock. A common side effect of opioids is constipation. To prevent it, she had a standing order for a laxative that in her case caused explosive diarrhea. When the nurse made her medication rounds and started to open Mia's prescribed laxative, even though Mia desperately needed something, she refused it. When the nurse asked why, Mia managed to get across to her that the diarrhea was just too much. The nurse just stood there and stared, and so I intervened. "Whatever happened to old fashioned natural remedies like prune juice?" I asked. She quickly replied "The laxative works faster and she doesn't need to go another day without having a bowel movement." I understood and had to remind myself that hospitals do good work, but they also prescribe pills. If Mia was going to get an old fashioned remedy like prune juice for constipation, I was going to be the one to insist on it.

In the meantime, since the constipation had Mia feeling miserable, I told her to go ahead and take the laxative. But I also told the nurse that this would be the last time. Of course, a few minutes later Mia had diarrhea, not just one time, but three. Not only did it clean her out, but it also wiped her out, leaving her feeling drained. After that day, she had a prune and apple juice cocktail every morning before breakfast. We also agreed that she could have whatever she wanted for breakfast, but she had to eat a bowl of raisin bran first. Just as I knew it would, the remedy worked. No more laxatives; no more diarrhea.

OUR GRATITUDE LESSON: There is a reason that home remedies have stood the test of time; they work. Imagine how much better off we would be if healthy eating became mainstream and dispensing chemicals in the form of pills was secondary.

YOUR GRATITUDE STORY: What home remedies have you used that worked?

January 27

Laughter

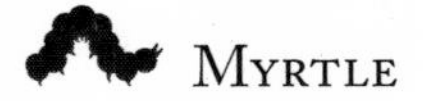 Myrtle

Mia's catheter was removed today, so we decided to start a cranberry juice regimen to help prevent urinary tract infections, another home remedy. She didn't need any more pills and definitely didn't want to have to have the catheter reinserted. She tried the cranberry juice and liked it, so she charmed one of the technicians into keeping her stocked up without me knowing it. They even had a secret stash, or so they thought.

It was late afternoon, and Mia had just come back from therapy and settled in for the evening. I headed to the cafeteria to see what they were serving for dinner and ran into the technician with both hands full of cranberry juice. She pretended that she was bringing them to Mia to choose the flavor she liked best. I turned around and followed her back to the room and she started to tell Mia what she had told me, but the way she explained it didn't make sense. Mia had a guilty look on her face. "You guys are busted!" I said. The three of us started laughing and couldn't stop. The technician was bent over holding her stomach. Mia laughed so hard that she started pointing to her head, indicating that the laughter was making her head hurt. And I just flopped down on the bed, holding my stomach. Finally, the technician explained that Mia's plan was to drink as much as she wanted, whenever she wanted, and I was not to know anything about it. They both knew I wouldn't approve of her drinking all the juice she wanted to drink. She didn't need the extra calories. For several days, whenever I ran into the technician, we laughed.

OUR GRATITUDE LESSON: Laughter is a drug with no harmful side effects. A good dose is a powerful weapon against any disease.

YOUR GRATITUDE STORY: List five things or people that always make you laugh.

January 28

Big Brothers

Myrtle

Mia dreaded getting up early, but not today; Cameron was headed home to spend the weekend with her and she could hardly wait. She'd been thinking about it all week. He would be taking her to therapy, and she'd get to show him her progress. She was also eager for the therapists to meet him, since she had already told them about his work as a trainer and strength and conditioning coach.

Her weekend therapy schedule was light, so he could work with her one-on-one. He was amazed at the progress she'd made since his last visit. She could turn her head to the right and actually keep it there for a few minutes. He noticed how her vision was improving in her right eye. She could push the "call" button for assistance, and even though it took her a couple of minutes, she could speak well enough to let the nurse know what she needed. Cameron cut her hair, another thing she was proud to say that her big brother could do. For dinner of course she got to choose the restaurant. He placed the order and went and picked it up. They ended the day with him watching sports. Mia didn't like TV, but she tolerated it for her big brother.

On Sunday afternoon, a couple of their college friends from Chattanooga visited. Mia was shocked. "How ...they... know...bout... me?" she asked Cameron. "Some of my homies in Chatt got the word around, he replied. "Wow... they .... all this... way ....to see me?" she asked. "Yeap, you're special," he replied. When they left, Mia and Cameron talked about their college days and the friends they'd made and how the friendships had lasted all this time.

It was a one-of-a-kind weekend. Cameron had never spent that much time in a hospital, so it was almost as much therapeutic for him as it was for Mia. It strengthened their brother-sister bond. Before Cameron left, we joined hands, prayed together, and shed some cleansing tears.

OUR GRATITUDE LESSON: When it comes to family, no one can replace a parent, but there's just something about a sibling that always sticks with you and ought to make you thankful.

YOUR GRATITUDE STORY: How many siblings do you have? List one special thing you like about each one of them.

January 30

A Dying Friend

 Myrtle

We had received word that our friend Marvin had died and Mia woke up with him and his family on her mind. We met the Johnson and Williams families when we moved to New York in 1979, just a few weeks after Mia was born. We became friends and kept in contact over the years.

"Mama…is…funeral…now?" she asked. "Not yet," I told her. "Man" she said with a long pause, "I… hate we ….can't go. That su.., su…, you know what I mean, not good," she said, growing somewhat frustrated, because she couldn't say "that sucks." I assured her that the family understood our situation and wanted to be here with us as well.

We talked about our last Thanksgiving trip to New York in 2016, a trip we had taken for the last six years. It was the first one we had taken without Cameron. The atmosphere was not as celebratory, yet we were grateful to be there. Marvin had been placed on hospice care just a few days before we arrived, so we wanted to be there to do whatever we could to help make his final days as comfortable as possible. We arrived on the Wednesday before Thanksgiving, just about 30 minutes before the hospice nurse arrived, so Mia was able to help get things set up. For the three days we were there, Mia was vigilant with Marvin. She checked his vitals, did what she could to make him comfortable, and showed his daughter Sharon how to set up his pain meds. Marvin still had his sense of humor and told his family that he liked having his own private nurse, who was much better at taking care of him than they were. When we got ready to leave, he gave Mia a silver dollar from his coin collection. It was his way of saying "thank you."

Knowing that it would be the last time we would see Marvin alive, we gave the family our word that we would be back to be with them during the funeral, so not being able to attend left us not only feeling sad, but helpless as well. Nonetheless, we still had some things to add to our gratitude lists. I was grateful that Mia remembered Marvin's death and that she had asked me to help her say a special prayer for the family. We prayed together and talked about how good it felt to be able to spend time with him during his final Thanksgiving days. We were grateful to be there to support the family and that technology had allowed us to keep in touch after we left.

OUR GRATITUDE LESSON: The dead are not dead unless you forget them. Hold fast to the good memories.

YOUR GRATITUDE STORY: If you could bring back three people from the dead, who would they be and why?

February 1

Answers

MYRTLE

My doctor and co-workers knew what I needed before I even asked. They advised me to request a year of intermittent medical leave, something I hadn't even had time to think about. I immediately completed the paperwork and once it was approved, I could work part-time while Mia was in therapy. Having caring, considerate, and knowledgeable people on your team during a crisis is invaluable.

OUR GRATITUDE LESSON: And it shall come to pass, that before they call, I will answer; and while they are yet speaking, I will hear. KJV – Isaiah 65:24.

YOUR GRATITUDE STORY: Think of a time when you experienced a crisis. Who were the people that stepped in to help you get through it? Did you thank them?

February 2

Social Security Disability Benefits

 Myrtle

Completing the paperwork for Social Security disability was tough. Every question on every page was a painful reminder that these questions were usually completed by an older person and not by the "disabled person," my 37-year-old daughter had become. There were 35 pages of questions about her daily routine, what she was doing before she had the stroke, how the stroke had affected her personal care, her interests, hobbies, and social activities. They asked about her abilities: Could she stand, lift, squat? How long could she pay attention? Was she using a wheelchair, cane, crutches or other supportive devices?

Tears blurred my vision as I did my best to answer each question, sometimes having to pause to refocus. I knew I had to get through them in order to get her the help she desperately needed and deserved. I also knew I had to answer each question truthfully. Some questions were redundant, and to lie was to set Mia up to be denied benefits. I remembered that there were places in this world where applying for financial assistance is not an option, so I completed the application one question and one issue at a time. Before placing it in the return envelope, I knew it would be wise to make copies to keep for our records. This would not be the last time I would have to answer these questions, so having a copy would make the next application a bit easier.

GRATITUDE LESSON: The words "social security" are most often associated with the elderly. To live in a country where assistance is available at any age is not something to be taken lightly.

YOUR GRATITUDE STORY: List five ways you have benefited from government services.

February 3

Student Loans

 MYRTLE

Mia's bills were piling up. I wasn't excited about dealing with her creditors but I decided to take them on, one at a time, starting with her student loans. She'd been making payments regularly, but at this point, I had to look at her options. I contacted the Department of Education and learned that I could apply to have her loans discharged if the Social Security Administration (SSA) determined that she was disabled. Since I didn't have the password to access her account online, I asked them to snail mail me the paperwork. I received it a few days later, completed it, and stuck it back in the mail. I could check this task off my list and wait for the outcome.

OUR GRATITUDE LESSON: In America every willing individual has a shot at a formal education, regardless of ability to pay. There are people who are literally dying to get here to take advantage of such an opportunity.

YOUR GRATITUDE STORY: Use the Internet and find five countries that do not offer student loans, countries where education has to be paid for out-of-pocket.

February 9

Taxes

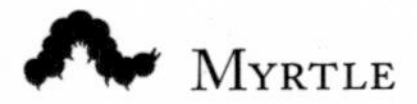 MYRTLE

The next debt collector on the list was the Internal Revenue Service (IRA), a debt collector that no one likes to tackle. Mia owed back taxes on a business she had co-owned. Up until now, she had been making monthly payments.

I made the first dreaded call and ended up being put on hold for an hour and 15 minutes, only to be told that I needed to go online and download and complete a form giving them permission to discuss her case with me. It wasn't the answer I wanted to hear, but it was a part of the process, so I had to do it. Thankful in advance for computers, the Internet, fax machines, and scanners, I began completing and submitting the forms, and after three more phone calls, her payments were suspended. I was relieved. It was not an easy process but it was worthwhile.

OUR GRATITUDE LESSON: Were it not for paying taxes, Social Security disability would not have been an option. We still had plenty to be thankful for.

YOUR GRATITUDE STORY: Everyone who has worked and paid taxes has an IRS story. What's yours? Did it have a happy or sad ending? There is something to be grateful for in both cases.

February 10

Assistive Devices

 MYRTLE

Today Mia got her very own four-pronged walker, a walker that she was proud of. She had it parked beside her bed where her wheelchair used to be, so I would be sure to see it when I came into the room. Her wheelchair was stationed in the hallway right next to her door, where she said it was going to stay during the day. She wanted to use the cane as much as she could. Cameron was coming to see her this weekend and she couldn't wait to show it to him. Tonight she could add "my own cane" to her gratitude list.

OUR GRATITUDE LESSON: Whether it be to improve mobility, vision, mental capacity, hearing, or learning, at some point in life we all need at least one assistive device. Give thanks for the devices and the people who make them.

YOUR GRATITUDE STORY: List the assistive devices you use now or have had to use in the past.

February 14

Valentines

Myrtle

Today is Valentine's Day. Last night I went to the store and bought miniature boxes of chocolates and put them in a basket for Mia to give to "special" staff. She liked the idea and enjoyed handing them out on the first and second shifts. It was a pleasant surprise for the staff, and Mia was also surprised at how good it felt. She commented that it was just a little box of candy but "they acted like it was something big." I reminded her that when you give from the heart, it always feels good to both the giver and receiver, that the size of the gift was not as important.

Mia also received several Valentine treats, enough to fill the basket she had emptied. Her night nurse brought her a large Hershey's kiss. Family members brought her treats. She even received a handmade Valentine card and cash from a cousin she barely knew in another state. And her Uncle Raymond who rarely buys gifts for anyone surprised her with a Valentine blanket and heart-shaped pillow. She adored the pillow and showed it to every person that came into her room. When she finally wound down for the night, she tested the pillow and said it was a perfect fit for her stitched-up head. "It's right. for…me…for my…head, you know…what…I mean," she said to me. The stitches from the surgery meant she could only sleep on her right side, so the pillow was just the right size. She asked me to place the blanket at the foot of the bed and to keep it there, even when she was out of the room. To this day, she still sleeps on that pillow and takes it with her on overnight trips.

The next day she woke up with Valentine thoughts on her mind. She looked over at her basket of treats and thanked me for the idea and once again mentioned how good it felt. What she didn't know but would learn in the days ahead was that it felt equally as good to me.

OUR GRATITUDE LESSON: Giving and receiving are two sides of the same coin.

YOUR GRATITUDE STORY: If you had a million dollars to give away, list five people you would give it to? Why?

February 20

Jigsaw Puzzles

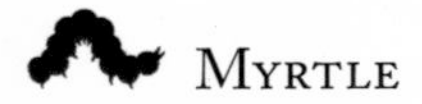 MYRTLE

Puzzles are highly recommended for stroke patients. In theory they are an inexpensive way to help the brain to begin developing new neural pathways. Even for individuals who have not had their brains compromised by a stroke or other catastrophic illness, puzzles are therapeutic. The occupational therapist had shown Mia a couple of jigsaw puzzles, and Mia asked me what I thought about them. I told her that I thought it was a good idea and could be a fun way to help her brain heal a little faster, so she was willing to give them a try. Today she finished her first one, which was a 48-piece puzzle. Even though she said it made her head hurt, she was proud of herself and couldn't wait to share the good news with her therapist. She would later move on to Word Search, which has been another inexpensive tool to improve her reading and writing skills and help to rewire her brain.

OUR GRATITUDE LESSON: Solving a jigsaw puzzle is like solving life's problems: it helps to first look at the big picture. Then value each piece.

YOUR GRATITUDE STORY: If you could design a jigsaw puzzle of one person, who would it be? How many pieces would your puzzle contain?

February 22

Disappointment

MYRTLE

Today we got the news that Mia would be going home in a week; the news came from one of her therapists. When she brought Mia back from her session, she asked me if anyone had mentioned it to me. Mention it? I couldn't believe it. "Wait a minute," I said to her. "It was my understanding that a health care team would sit down with us to discuss discharge plans. So where's the team?" She was young, and I could tell that my question and tone of voice, and probably my facial expression all made her a bit uncomfortable. "I'll have the doctor's assistant come and talk to you, and maybe she can answer your questions," she replied. "No," I said, "I want to speak to the doctor. Is he on the floor today?" She left the room saying she would check to see but she never returned. Mia later confirmed that I had indeed made her uncomfortable with my questions.

I didn't want to believe that this was the way the hospital discharged patients. I later learned that a team sets the discharge date, but they don't include the patient or the family in the discussion. What I got was a minute or two of a staff member's time, and that person talked to me while standing. No one sat down and talked to me about anything. It turned out that my expectations were unrealistic.

I was angry, and some of it had to do with the fact that I was not ready for Mia to go home. I didn't feel that she was where I wanted her to be in terms of recovery. She had been in the hospital for two months recovering from a massive stroke that left her needing total care at home, and that was no simple feat. I was frustrated because I needed more time to get things set up. We needed equipment for her bathroom and bedroom. Furniture needed to be moved out of the house and things rearranged. She needed a wheelchair. And there were other things that needed to be taken care of. Had the rehab team not taken those things into consideration? I understood that they had to move patients in and out in a timely fashion, but the least they could do was give a family advance notice.

A day later, while Mia was in therapy, the doctor stopped by the room to let me know that he'd heard about my dissatisfaction with Mia's discharge date. He explained, while standing, that it really didn't matter if she stayed another week or two; there wouldn't be a big improvement because her rehab would take months. I told him that I understood that much, but I would have appreciated being told this in advance. Of course he didn't budge from his position. He also reminded me that the insurance company had the final say, and Mia's days were numbered; her time was about to be up. When he left, I closed the door and cried, but not for long. I'm not one for pity parties. I had to keep looking ahead.

OUR GRATITUDE LESSON: Life brings disappointment. Thank God in advance that it doesn't become discouragement.

YOUR GRATITUDE STORY: What has been one of your greatest disappointments? What lesson did you learn from it?

February 27

Resources

 Myrtle

I began asking questions and looking around for the equipment we needed. The right people, places, and things started showing up. A co-worker told me about local organizations that should be able to assist me. I contacted two of them and learned that they both offered services to assist persons with disabilities to regain independence. I made appointments. It felt good to walk through their doors and sit down and talk to staff members who treated you with compassion. I left the first one with the equipment Mia needed for her bed, and I left the second one with a promise that they would work with Mia to help get her back to as much independence as possible. I had two new organizations to add to my gratitude list.

OUR GRATITUDE LESSON: Nearly every moment of every day, we have the opportunity to give something to someone else: our time, our love, and our gifts. – S. Truett Cathy

YOUR GRATITUDE STORY: List five things you would like to do before you die.

March 1

Social Workers

Determined to find long term care for Mia outside the nursing home, I went online and found information on the state's Traumatic Brain Injury Program. After making a couple of phone calls, I discovered that they had an office in the hospital, actually right around the corner from Mia's room. No one on her rehab team had mentioned it to me, which led me to wonder how many of them knew it was there.

I made an appointment to meet with the program's social worker. One of the first questions she asked me was if anyone from the hospital had told me about a long-term care rehab hospital in Georgia that offered services to individuals with traumatic brain injuries. Of course, my answer was no, and she reacted as if it was no surprise. She explained their services and admission policy and said that she would be glad to submit an application on Mia's behalf. I signed papers giving her permission to make the application. She also told me about a program called CHOICES, a long-term service and support program for adults age 21 and older with a physical disability, and gave me a contact number to call to see if Mia qualified for the program. I took her card and left her office feeling better. I was grateful that she had pointed me in the right direction.

OUR GRATITUDE LESSON: A "social worker" is more than a job title, it's a calling. When you're in crisis and find someone who has the compassion not only to listen, but to act, it's a blessing.

YOUR GRATITUDE STORY: Reach out to a social worker, any social worker, and thank her or him for their service. If you think you don't know any, start with any social service agency like the Department of Human Services (DHS) or the Department of Children's Services (DCS). Social workers rarely get the thanks they deserve. Don't forget to journal about how good it made you feel to reach out.

March 2

Goodbyes

MYRTLE

It was time to leave rehab and head home. Mia said her goodbyes to her favorite hospital staff. They all wished her well and commented on how they had not seen a patient make the progress she'd made in such a short period of time. They mentioned how they liked her bubbly personality and how she brought a spirit of light-hearted cheer to the room for both staff and patients. She had a way of keeping them laughing and keeping the therapists on their toes. Her doctor called her progress unusual and commented that he was glad to see her personality shine through. He had seen some patients leave the hospital feeling apathetic and sometimes without hope.

After Mia made her last "goodbye" rounds, it was time to take the next steps; steps that we both knew we had to face with a positive attitude. Raymond and Warren were there before 9:00 a.m. to help us get packed up. Two of Mia's therapists helped her to the car. Shortly after beginning therapy she had set a goal to walk out of the hospital, and with assistance, she did. It was a long stretch from her room to the parking garage so she wasn't able to walk the entire distance, but she was determined to walk part of the way. A big milestone!

We got about a quarter mile down the road in the car and Mia motioned that she had to throw up. I had put a couple of plastic bags in the glove compartment, so I pulled into a restaurant parking lot, grabbed a bag, and handed it to her. She put it up to her mouth and I took off again. We managed to make it home without her vomiting.

Dwight met us at home, and he and Raymond unloaded the car and helped get things set up in her bedroom, starting with the equipment I had picked up from one of the non-profit organizations. They didn't know how to install it so Mia showed them. She had seen similar equipment in some of her patients' homes and at the hospital. Once we got things set up, Dwight took some rugs and a few things to our storage unit and left us to get settled in, to begin the next leg of the journey.

Mia's first night at home went well. She didn't even get up to use the bathroom. Before going to sleep, she mentioned how good it felt to lie down in her own bed for the first time in almost two months. I think I was awake every hour or two to see if she needed anything. We were off to a good start, and like being in any marathon I knew I had to pace myself. I was grateful to remember that this day marked the beginning of another phase of healing. We were moving on.

OUR GRATITUDE LESSON: Even when leaving is the best option, endings are a little bit sad and beginnings are a little bit scary. Be grateful for both.

YOUR GRATITUDE STORY: What's the hardest "goodbye" you ever had to make? Describe it and the new beginning.

March 3

Motorized Shopping Carts

Myrtle

Other than commenting on what we called "lazy people" who used motorized shopping carts but looked like they were able to push a regular cart around the grocery store, neither Mia nor I had ever given much thought to motorized shopping carts. Time brings about a change.

Today would be Mia's first time using a motorized shopping cart, and she quickly learned that it takes some getting used to. She dragged things and bumped into things, including other people's carts. She hit one gentleman's cart, upsetting him to the point that he yelled at her. His yelling didn't sit well with me, but I ended up laughing about it because Mia never even knew she hit him; neither had she heard him yelling. Her peripheral vision in her right eye was gone so not noticing things on her right side was normal for her. She was on to the next aisle when I told her that she had run into the gentleman.

We finished shopping and managed to leave the store without Mia's falling or causing any major damage. It would take her several more trips to master driving the cart. This first experience was all we needed to change our attitudes about motorized carts and the people who use them. It wasn't as easy as it looked, and if it were not for the carts, she wouldn't have been able to shop. She would have had to stay in the car or maybe sit in the front of the store and wait while I shopped. Until now, none of that had ever crossed our minds.

OUR GRATITUDE LESSON: Something as simple as a motorized shopping cart taught us to challenge assumptions. Regardless of the reasons people use them, for us they made shopping so much easier.

YOUR GRATITUDE STORY: Have you ever made unkind remarks about people on motorized shopping carts? The next time you see one, don't judge because you don't know their story. Offer to help instead.

March 4

Acts of Kindness

 MYRTLE

We went out for dinner, and the experience brought on a couple of scares. Mia made it from the car to the restaurant just fine but when we got to the table, she lost her balance. My nursing skills kicked in and I kept her from hitting the floor, but the accident drew stares from other diners, stares that made Mia feel more uneasy. Once we sat down at the table, she turned over a glass of water. More stares. The glass was sitting on her right side, which meant she didn't see it when she sat down.

We had a kind waitress who did her best to assure Mia that everything was okay. By the time we got our food, Mia was feeling a little better, so we sat quietly and enjoyed the meal. When we finished, she strapped on her helmet and we headed for the door, but Mia lost her balance and again and I was able to I brace her fall. This time the greeter noticed and offered to walk us to the car. Mia thanked her.

As she buckled her seatbelt, Mia mentioned how uncomfortable she felt with people staring at her because of her helmet, the near falls, and spilling water at the table. I encouraged her to look at it as special attention that she would not ordinarily get. I told her that this was her first time dining out since she had the stroke, and even though it wasn't easy, things would get better with time. I gave her a challenge: "Tonight when you work on your gratitude list, see how many things you have to be grateful for as a result of eating out today, even those you think are bad." Without my help, she thought of four: she didn't hurt herself; she had her helmet on to protect her head; she had a kind waitress; and she had a kind greeter.

OUR GRATITUDE LESSON: No act of kindness is ever too small.

YOUR GRATITUDE STORY: For a week, do something kind for seven different people and each day journal about how it felt.

March 6

Outpatient Therapists

Myrtle

Mia had established quite a bond with the hospital therapists, however she didn't know what to expect on her first day of outpatient therapy at a new facility with all new faces. Day one turned out to be good. When I picked her up, she talked about how much she liked her speech therapist, who gave her homework on the first day. She said he was funny and, "he acts like he cares," which is always a plus for any patient regardless of the environment. She was off to a good start.

OUR GRATITUDE LESSON: People don't care what you know until they know that you care.

YOUR GRATITUDE STORY: Who are three people who care about you? Do something to let them know that you appreciate them before it's too late.

March 8

Mix-Matched Shoes

 Myrtle

In order to prevent her right foot from dragging when she walked, a term referred to as "foot drop" in the stroke world, Mia had been discharged from the hospital wearing a foot brace. In order for the brace to fit properly, one shoe had to be larger than the other, which meant buying new sneakers. She wore a size 8 ½ but needed a 10 ½ for her right foot. We could buy two pairs of shoes so that they matched, or buy one pair, which meant they wouldn't match. For now she opted for mix-match shoes. She was grateful to be able to walk; the fashion statement didn't matter.

OUR GRATITUDE LESSON:

> *You have brains in your head.*
> *You have feet in your shoes.*
> *You can steer yourself*
> *any direction you choose.*
>
> *Dr. Seuss*

YOUR GRATITUDE STORY: List three compliments you receive on a regular basis? How many of them have to do with your physical appearance?

March 9

"Thank You" Notes

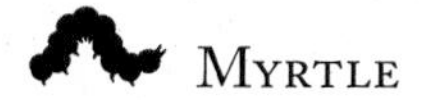 MYRTLE

Now that we were settled in at home, I wanted to thank the people who had been so kind to us during Mia's hospital stay so I decided to send them "thank you" cards. I shared my idea with Mia and she was all for it. This would be a chance to catch two fish with one worm: She would begin her gratitude practice again, and I would strengthen mine. I always kept plenty of "thank you" cards on hand, and so we got started right away. The stroke had attacked the language center in Mia's left brain, wiping out all memory of the alphabet and the ability to spell. She didn't even recognize her name on paper. Because she had no movement in her right hand, I had to hold the card in place as she copied her name which I had written on a blank piece of paper. Signing her name to each card was a slow process that reminded her once again of things she couldn't do as a result of the stroke. But she would not be defeated. Each day I wrote the message and she signed a few cards. By the fourth day, she was thanking me for the challenge.

OUR GRATITUDE LESSON: There are two kinds of gratitude: the sudden kind you feel when you receive something, and the deeper kind you feel when you give.

YOUR GRATITUDE STORY: Fill in the blank: I feel grateful when ___________________.

March 10

A Shower

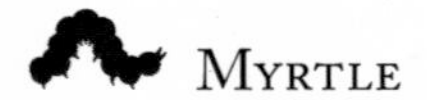 Myrtle

New shower fixtures had to be installed in Mia's bathroom: hand rails, a shower head with a rope type sprayer, and a waterproof adjustable shower chair. Cousin Pearl had given her a brand new shower chair. Dwight picked up the other fixtures and installed them. In her own jumbled words she thanked her uncle and told him what a good handyman he was. "Glad to do it," he replied and told her to go ahead and test the shower.

It was her first shower since leaving the hospital. With her helmet in place and holding tight to the new handrail, she cautiously stepped into the tub, hoping that her right leg wouldn't buckle without the brace. She looked to me for reassurance, and I gave her a nod and extended my hand just in case she needed it. Positioning herself in front of the chair, she plopped down with a sigh. She turned the water on and adjusted the temperature, then grabbed the shower head and allowed the warm water to soak her face and trickle down her body. Smiling, she looked at me and told me I could leave. "I'll call…when…I want…help," she said. Hesitantly, I left her alone.

When she called me back to help her finish up she told me how good the shower felt. However to my surprise, she spoke of how grateful she was to all the people who made it possible for her to be able to sit down and take a shower at home. She also mentioned how being in the shower reminded her of the day she had the stroke; the bathroom is where it all began.

OUR GRATITUDE LESSON: I used to think of a shower as only a necessity. Today, I see it as a luxury, a luxury that is the result of being showered with so many blessings. I will never again take it for granted. -Mia

YOUR GRATITUDE STORY: How would your life change if you couldn't take a shower or bath for a week, a month, two months?

March 11

Remembering the Stroke

Myrtle

"Mama, I... remember...the....stroke," Mia shouted right in the middle of dinner. I almost dropped my fork. "I know...what...happened. It was... the...bathroom," she began telling me. She was anxious, almost like she was thinking faster than she could speak. Her words didn't flow the way she wanted them to flow, but that didn't stop her from sharing. Here is a modified summary of her recollection.

"I was in the bathroom putting hairspray on my hair, and there was a thick cloud of spray. Then I got dizzy and fell. I don't know if I hit my head on something, but I kept trying to get up but I couldn't. I could move my left side, so I started pushing myself with my left leg and sliding toward my bed. I thought about my phone on the bed, and I got close enough to the bed to grab the bedspread. I pulled it off the bed, but I didn't see my phone. I was really hot and sweating a lot. I tried to get up again so I could turn my fan around to blow on me, but I couldn't get up. I could touch the base of the fan and pulled on it until it fell over, and then I could feel the cool air blowing on my face. Mama I was scared. I just started praying. I was saying 'God please let my Mama come home so I won't die.' You just don't know how scared I was Mama, and how hard I prayed for you to come home because I knew that you didn't always come straight home after work."

I shared with her how I had planned to go to buy yarn and changed my mind in the middle of the parking lot and headed home. I told her that I believed it was divine intervention that led me home. She agreed. This was the 62nd day after the stroke, and her memory was returning. It was another indicator that her brain was rewiring itself. Was it time spent in the shower yesterday that triggered her memory? Hmmmm....

OUR GRATITUDE LESSON: What is hard to endure is often sweet to recall. Rejoice!

YOUR GRATITUDE STORY: List five things you want to remember for as long as you live.

March 12

Learning To Write My Name

 MYRTLE

We mailed out five "thank you" cards each day. I wrote the message, and Mia had to sign each card. "Mama, how do you spell my name, I forgot?" she asked. "M... I... A," I answered slowly, hoping she would get it. "How do you make an 'M,'" she asked? I wrote 'M I A' in large letters and she did her best to make her letters look like mine, but she couldn't. They were squiggly and going downhill; none of them were the same size. After the first card, she looked at it and laughed. "Lord, I...can't...even...know ...to....write...my...name. How.....to...spell...it...again? I laughed with her, although deep inside I was sad and wanted to burst into tears. Even when she managed to draw the letters on paper, she didn't know what she was writing since she didn't recognize the alphabet. All I could do was tell her that in time she would get better.

Later that night after she went to bed and the cards lay on the table ready to be mailed, I looked at them and this time I let the tears flow. I thought about how she had been an honor student, gone to college, and here she was, 37 years old, unable to recognize or spell her name. The stroke had erased every bit of what she had learned. All we had to hold on to is hope that the loss would be temporary.

OUR GRATITUDE LESSON: "All I really need to know, I learned in Kindergarten." -Robert Fulghum

YOUR GRATITUDE STORY: List one Kindergarten lesson that you never forgot.

March 13

Medical Bills and Bad Credit

 Myrtle

Mia's medical bills kept coming in, so I sat down and created a template to send to her creditors. I thanked them for their services and explained that Mia had no source of income and therefore wasn't able to pay them right now. I also asked for their patience which I knew didn't mean much in the business world, but for now it was the best I could do. I made copies and each time she received a bill, I inserted the provider's name and sent them a letter. It didn't stop the bills but I felt better. After all, the bills meant she had received the services and in this case, those services had kept her alive. My gratitude compelled me to at least honor the debt. I thought about how it would be if we lived in a country where those who received medical care and did not pay were detained as prisoners, sometimes indefinitely.

I began making monthly payments on her small bills. The larger ones would have to wait. I knew not paying them would ruin her credit, but I'd recently read somewhere that America had a bad credit score, so hers would fit right in. I did what I could and didn't feel badly about it. There were more pressing issues that demanded my attention.

OUR GRATITUDE LESSON: If you can't pay your bills, there's still a reason to be grateful: It means that someone trusted you enough to provide you with services.

YOUR GRATITUDE STORY: Make a list of everyone that you owe and why you owe them.

March 15

Choices

 MYRTLE

I had received notice that Mia would receive her last short-term disability check from her employer this week. This meant that terminating her health insurance would be next. I'd also received a call from the Social Security Administration saying that a determination on her disability application would not be made until April or May. Now what? Without insurance, would the neurosurgeon do the surgery to replace the piece of her skull that he'd removed to save her life? Would the surgery be scheduled before the SSA made a decision? Would she be able to continue to see her primary care doctor? How would we pay for medication? I didn't have any doubt that the determination would be in her favor; if anyone was disabled, Mia was. But it was the middle of March and "sometime in April or May" was a ways off; so what would we do in the meantime? I didn't have answers, but what I did have was the determination to keep believing that things would work out in our favor. I had to keep searching for services and get through each day with a smile, for me and for Mia.

Thanks to information I'd received earlier from the social worker with the Traumatic Brain Injury Program, I had an appointment with a care coordinator with CHOICES, a program that offers community-based services for adults 21 years of age and older with a physical disability. CHOICES would help a disabled person with daily living activities in their home as well as allow them to work and be actively involved in their local community. Like most government assistance programs, there were income and other restrictions: your assets couldn't value over a certain amount, and you couldn't have given away or sold anything for less than what it's worth in the last five years. With no income, Mia met the income guidelines, and she certainly qualified medically. She needed the level of care provided in a nursing home setting and would likely be receiving SSA disability.

The initial visit with CHOICES care coordinator lasted over an hour. She asked lots of repetitive questions, similar to those asked on the SSA's disability application. Nobody likes the drill of repetitive questions, but

I knew I had to jump through the hoops if I wanted the services that Mia desperately needed, and deserved. After we completed the application, I was told that if Mia qualified for the services, it would be June or July before they started. There would also be at least two more interviews. Another long wait, but I could see that answers were coming. I had put the ball in motion so I needed to be patient, be grateful, and keep moving. I also needed to add CHOICES to my gratitude list.

OUR GRATITUDE LESSON: Be careful when you pray for patience. The only way to know you have it is to be tested. Endure the test.

YOUR GRATITUDE STORY: Describe one time that your patience was tested. How did things turn out?

March 16

Co-Workers

 MYRTLE

Mia was now going to therapy three days a week for three hours a day, so during that time I went back to work. I can't say enough about how grateful I am for a job with good benefits including Intermittent Family Medical Leave Act (FMLA) and the best co-workers anyone could have. My job offered all employees the same basic benefits, but I had so much more. I had a compassionate supervisor. I worked with a team of people who put themselves in my shoes and said to me: "Take the time you need and do what you have to do for your daughter, we have your back." As hard as it was for me to process Mia's stroke, it would have been even harder if I had not had a work family that cared. I could not thank them enough.

OUR GRATITUDE LESSON: Compassionate people go beyond understanding your pain. They know what to do, when to do, and how to do it.

YOUR GRATITUDE STORY: List one time that you received help from compassionate co-workers. List one time when you have been a compassionate co-worker.

March 17

Change

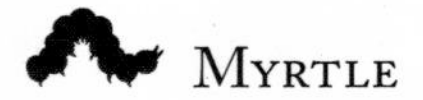 Myrtle

I went into the office, turned on my computer, and saw that my emails looked different, new software had been installed. I didn't like it and I didn't need it, not now of all times. There was nothing wrong with the old system, so why did they have to go and change it? I immediately went to a co-worker's office to vent and ask her to help me figure out this new system. Mastering the use of technology is not one of my strengths, so it didn't take much to frustrate me. On this particular morning I let it show big time. As my co-worker and I walked back over to my office, she reminded me that she relied on me to be calm, and since I was upset, I was upsetting her. I didn't pay her comment much attention. She showed me how to navigate the new system and went back to her office. I thanked her and as I sat wading through emails, I thought about what she had said.

I got up and went back over to her office and told her how I appreciated the reminder that I was always the one encouraging the team that there was never anything worth panicking over. Never. "Myrtle, I have never seen you react that way," she said to me. It went without saying that a lot of my reaction had to do with Mia, and the changes on the computer were nothing in comparison. We ended up laughing, and as always, the laughter felt good.

Change is always challenging whether it's for good or bad, but it's the one constant that we all must experience. The sooner we embrace it, the better off we are. Resisting and complaining won't improve things. I appreciated the candid reminder from a co-worker and moved on with my day.

OUR GRATITUDE LESSON: If you don't like something, change it. If you can't change it, change your attitude. -Maya Angelou

YOUR GRATITUDE STORY: List one change you've had to adjust to over the last year. Did you learn a lesson?

March 18

Her Daddy's Genes

 MYRTLE

I turned on the vacuum cleaner, and it didn't work. I told Mia that we needed a new one. "Bring… it…," she motioned to me, sitting on the edge of the couch. She asked me to help her turn it over so she could look at it. "It's torn up," I told her. "There is nothing you can do with it." She ignored me as she examined it. I moved on with my chores, and after a while I heard her calling me. I went back into the living room, and she said it was ready and asked me to plug it in. I did. She clicked the "on" switch and the vacuum cleaner worked. She looked at me and smirked. "My… daddy…taught… me …that," she said. "You're right," I replied. "You definitely didn't get it from me. I was ready to throw it away." We laughed. She told me that the next time something was broken to bring it to her before deciding to trash it.

As my brother Bill always says about Mia's dad: "You know Thomas could take the engine out of a car and put it back in with one hand, and the engine would run." Maybe the "fix-it" part of Mia's brain was sharper after the stroke? Hmmmm…

OUR GRATITUDE LESSON: Your genes don't necessarily determine your destiny, but there are times when they can be a natural resource. Cherish them.

YOUR GRATITUDE STORY: What genes from your parents are you most proud of?

March 19

Reflections

 Myrtle

Today I took some time to reflect not only on what happened to Mia but what was happening to me. The day Mia had the stroke I was 44 days away from my 64th birthday, and this was not how I'd planned to spend it. These were supposed to be my golden years, and there was nothing "golden" about watching your 37-year-old daughter go from a vibrant independent woman to a dependent child. There was nothing "golden" about being thrown back into the "take charge" caregiver role once again, or so I thought. Hadn't I played that role enough? Hadn't I had my share of tough times?

I'd helped take care of my mother after she was diagnosed with Alzheimer's, watching the disease gnaw away at her brain, reversing the mother-daughter role. Gradually, she deteriorated from one of the strongest women I knew, to one who didn't know her name or recognize her children's faces. Two years after she made the transition, I also lost my two oldest brothers within a two-month time span, leaving me feeling like I needed to take charge. Growing up in a single parent household, I'd taken on the "big sister" role to my younger siblings at an early age. I'd had my share of struggles, but nothing compared to this. I desperately needed to make sense of it all. But I couldn't.

What I did manage to string together was that I had spent quite a bit of my time taking charge of situations. I went back to when I was eight years old when my younger brother, Dwight was born. He was the first of seven younger siblings born between 1961and 1969. On the day he was born, my older cousin Erma came to stay with us for a few days to help out. It was a tradition with my mom and her sisters that whenever a sister was temporarily off her feet, the oldest nieces stepped in to help out.

What I remember most about Erma's stay with us was that she had to go to the laundromat because we didn't have a washer and dryer, and I had to go with her, but I didn't mind. The laundromat was in a bustling part of town where people shopped and socialized, so going with her was something I looked forward to. Looking back, I think going anywhere and learning new things always excited me.

Years later, Erma and I laughed about those days, but I always noticed a seriousness about Erma; she would say that at the age of eight I knew as much as she did about what to do around the house, and sometimes I was the one telling her what to do. I told her it was because I lived there and was familiar with everything, but she didn't buy that explanation. "You were just a grown child, you always have been. You were younger than me but you sure didn't need me to tell you what to do," she would say.

Doing laundry was my favorite chore. There was something intriguing about washers and dryers. It probably had a lot to do with me watching Mama scrub the dirt out of our clothes on a scrub board in a round tin tub. She had let me try it a few times. It was hard, back-breaking, knuckle-bruising work that no one enjoyed. So loading clothes into a washer and watching it twist the dirt out and then letting the heat of the dryer toss them into shape was magic to my eight-year-old eyes. As the family grew from four to ten in less than eight years, we finally got our first used washing machine, and I actually looked forward to Mama going to work and leaving me in charge. It meant I could load the washer and let it work its magic. If the weather was warm, I hung the clothes on the line to dry. In the winter, I would hang them up on a makeshift clothesline in the kitchen and turn the oven up as high as it would go so they would dry. But once Mama found out what I was doing, my dangerously brilliant idea came to a halt. But I still liked doing laundry and to this day, it's my favorite household chore.

So I wondered if it was nature or nurture that made me a "take charge "person? Was it my choices, or choices other people made for me? I hadn't given it much thought until now and why now? The only answer I could come up with was here I was with this cross to bear once again. Maybe someday I would be wise enough to understand it.

OUR GRATITUDE LESSON: As baseball Hall of Famer Hank Aaron said when he was in a slump, feeling bad about his performance, or having trouble off the field, his motto was "keep swinging."

YOUR GRATITUDE STORY: Complete this sentence: When it comes to my life, I totally understand.

March 20

Neuroplasticity

 MYRTLE

Mia continued to do her best scribbling her name on "thank you" cards. She asked me how I remembered who to send all the cards to, and I told her that I had saved each one and kept track of everything that was happening in my journal.

"Maybe…I…need…to…journal. She remembered how I had always encouraged her to journal and she would always start but never stick with it. "I was… hard-headed," she mentioned. Yes you were I thought to myself, but didn't say it. She wasn't ready to hear that lecture. She told me that now she really wanted to journal but couldn't even write. I assured her that we would figure out a way to do it, so she asked me to get her journal off her bedside table, and she placed it and a pen in bed with her. When she was in the hospital, I had bought her a couple of preschool activity books to help her relearn her alphabet so she also asked me to get one of those books so she could try to spell what she wanted to write. I explained to her that journaling was not about spelling words correctly. It was her own personal property, so spelling didn't matter. For her it wasn't that simple. She didn't know where to begin when it came to spelling words, which meant I had my work cut out for me. I needed patience to keep encouraging her. It's what caregivers do, right? I would see to it that she not only learned to write but that she would also learn to read again.

I researched what happens to people who are forced to learn to use their non-dominant hand after a stroke and learned that through what is called neuroplasticity, the ability of the brain to rewire or reorganize itself after injury, she could improve her writing skills. Repetition was the key. The more she practiced, the better she would be. We both vowed to give it our best. Let the journaling begin!

OUR GRATITUDE LESSON: Two of the most powerful words ever uttered: "I can."

YOUR GRATITUDE STORY: Complete this sentence: I have been wanting to__________________for a long time but never did because____________________.

March 21

Patience

Myrtle

Finally, I received a letter from the IRS stating that I could call and discuss Mia's delinquent taxes. Up until now, she had done a good job of making monthly payments, so maybe that would get her some brownie points. I made the intimidating call and was placed on hold for 45 minutes, only to be told that I needed to go to the their website and download another form and fax or mail it in in order for them to make a decision about her case. The waiting game continued. Mia's stroke had put me in situations in which I had more time to "wait" than I ever imagined being able to tolerate.

OUR GRATITUDE LESSON: Patience and time are warriors, and sometimes it's hard to declare a winner.

YOUR GRATITUDE STORY: Describe a time when you had to wait for something. How did things turn out?

March 22

Fear

 MYRTLE

Mia has always had a low tolerance for pain. Prior to the stroke, she sometimes took 800 milligrams of ibuprofen when she experienced joint pain caused by lupus. Since the stroke, I was concerned about the hydrocodone and tramadol she was taking around the clock in the hospital, and how often she asked for it once she got home. She complained that the headaches got worse when she went to physical therapy, and I didn't believe that the pain was exaggerated. But I also knew how easy and quickly one could become addicted to opioids. I had read about young stroke patients who had become addicted, some of them mothers who could no longer care for their children. In Mia's case, not only did she have the headaches caused by the stroke, but she also had additional pain from the craniectomy, which would take months to heal. So how could I tell her that I understood her pain but didn't want her to become addicted? I was not in her shoes. Ultimately, I had to let go and trust that things would play out the way she said they would..."Mama, I won't get hooked," was what she said whenever I questioned her need for pain pills.

What you think about you may bring about, so I had to stop thinking about addiction; I had to let go of my fears and believe that in time the pain would pass.

OUR GRATITUDE LESSON: Thank God that everything comes to pass in its own time.

YOUR GRATITUDE STORY: Fear cuts both ways. List one time that doing the thing you feared paid off. List one time that doing the thing you feared got you into trouble.

March 23

A Hard-Headed Fall

 MYRTLE

Mia bent over to pick up something in the bathroom and hit the floor. I heard her, and I almost fell running downstairs to see what had happened. When I got there she looked up at me and said, "I… knew…better. Mama, I'm not hurt." I was relieved but upset that she had tried something she knew was dangerous. Thank God she was wearing her helmet and for the rods Dwight had installed in the bathroom that allowed her to pull herself up; otherwise, I would have had to call someone to help us. There wasn't much I could do as a result of ruptured discs in my neck, which were from an automobile accident years past.

When she got up we checked for bruises and she had one on her thigh which probably had a lot to do with bruising easily when one is on a daily dose of aspirin. We both knew it would take a while for the bruise to heal. Later, we laughed about the fall and the fact that even with a chunk of her skull missing, she was still hard headed. I reminded her of one of her grandmother's quotes: "A hard head makes a soft back-end." We laughed even harder.

OUR G RATITUDE LESSON: Life is like an EKG, without the ups and downs, you're not living. -Ed Young

YOUR GRATITUDE STORY: Growing up, what catchy phrases did your parents use when you were "hard-headed?"

March 24

$6 Glasses

Myrtle

Since the stroke had affected the vision in Mia's right eye, her prescription glasses didn't help at all. Actually, they made her head hurt, so she stopped wearing them. John, her speech therapist suggested reading glasses from the dollar store. When we left therapy, we stopped and picked up a pair for $6, and they worked. "That's…something," Mia remarked when she tried them on in the store. "Six dollars?" She couldn't believe it. She couldn't remember how much her prescription glasses cost, but she knew they were a lot more than $6. We talked about it all the way home. "Umph, John…know…what… he…." I finished the sentence for her. "Yes he did," I replied. He had given us a simple solution to what turned out to be a temporary problem.

OUR GRATITUDE LESSON: Not everything of value has to cost a lot.

YOUR GRATITUDE STORY: What is one thing that you recently purchased that cost a lot but turned out to have little value? What is one thing you recently purchased that cost a little and turned out to be of great value?

March 25

Sisters

 MYRTLE

April, my mother's niece, called today to check on Mia and to say that she and her sister, Carla, wanted to come over and stay with her for a day to give me a chance to run errands or take some time for myself. I took her up on the offer. It felt good to know that they were thinking about us, and it didn't take me long to remember why. As I mentioned earlier, it was a family tradition. They knew I needed help and so they did what our mothers had taught us to do: they stepped in to help.

Our mothers were sisters who enjoyed visiting each other, mostly sitting around laughing and talking, shelling peas, snapping beans, and eating. Mama was known for her good cooking, and their mother, Aunt Mae loved to eat, so any time she came to visit, food was a part of the visit, even if it was nothing more than a piece of cake. Their strong bond brought back vivid memories of the day Mama died. It was a Saturday evening. Cousins Dorothy and Martha had come over to cook dinner for us: fried catfish, spaghetti, and coleslaw, a family favorite. Aunt Mae had come earlier to spend some time with Mama.

When Dorothy and Martha started cooking, Aunt Mae moved to the kitchen and sat at the table while my sister and I went into the room to check on Mama. As her breathing slowed and became shallow, I knew that her body was beginning to shut down, so I went into the kitchen to let everyone know. "Aunt Mae, I think mama is leaving us," I said to her. She looked at me and replied in a matter of fact way, "Well Merl (she never called me Myrtle), we all have to leave here and if it's her time, she's at peace, in her own bed, and that's a good way to go." She then looked at Dorothy and asked when the fish would be ready. I thought to myself: Is that any way to respond to the news that your sister is taking her last breaths, the one that you had been so close to all your life?

Well, fast forward several years and I understand her reaction, or at least I think I do. What she said was the truth; we do all have to leave here, so it makes sense to live each day to the fullest so that there are no regrets at the end. For her that hot fish plate was just fine on the day that her sister died.

You see, Aunt Mae was the most candid of Mama's eight sisters. She was the one who always spoke her mind, sometimes with a twist of humor, but always with a straight face. She said what she meant and meant what she said. People often teased her about her eating habits - that she ate too many salty, artery-clogging foods. Her reply was always the same: "This is my body and my food. If it kills me, I'll die enjoying it, and I'll die full." She lived a vibrant 81 years. By example, she taught me a profound lesson: death is a certainty, so accept it and keep living. She had also taught her daughters April and Carla a few things about life, for which I was also grateful.

OUR GRATITUDE LESSON: "For the LORD is good; His mercy is everlasting; and His truth endureth to all generations." Psalms 100:5 KJV

YOUR GRATITUDE LESSON: Describe a special bond you have with your sister (or someone you feel especially close to). Have you told them how special they are?

March 26

Is Age More Than A Number?

 MYRTLE

I was at the office when my cell phone rang. It was Mia calling from physical therapy. In her 'little girl' voice and jumbled speech, she asked, "Mama…how…old…am I?" I paused, wondering who wanted to know. "You're 38, but who wants…?" Click went the phone before I could finish my question. Guess I would have to wait until I picked her up to find out.

When I got to the facility where she went for speech, occupational, and physical therapy to pick her up, Mia was standing outside talking to another young woman in her late twenties who also had had a stroke. She and the young lady had been in the hospital at the same time and therefore knew each other. They were discharged a week apart and ended up in therapy at the same time. The young lady's husband was standing with them and told me about their questions about their age. He smiled when I mentioned how Mia hung up the phone on me, and he explained that his wife and Mia had been talking about their strokes when his wife asked Mia how old she was and Mia didn't know so she called me to ask. His wife didn't know her age either, so she had to ask him. Neither of them seemed to be bothered about not knowing their age; they were just curious. But for me it was a bittersweet moment. Here were two young women with a combined age of less than 65, and neither of them knew when they were born. Mercy!

OUR GRATITUDE LESSON: If we could forget our troubles as easily as we forget our blessings, life would be so much better.

YOUR GRATITUDE LESSON: What age would you be if you didn't know how old you were? Why?

March 28

A Center for the Disabled

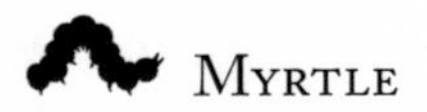

Myrtle

April and Carla came earlier than I expected today and told me to take as much time as I needed to run errands. I hit the road. My first stop was one of the organizations on my list of places to look for services. I wanted to learn more about their music therapy program, and see if I could get Mia enrolled. I had a gut feeling that it would make a profound difference in her recovery. I knew that the part of her brain that was damaged by the stroke could not be repaired, but I had read that the brain was capable of creating new pathways, and music could rewire the brain faster than anything else I had read about.

I arrived at the center and just a few minutes after signing in I sat down with staff who introduced me to their services. She told me that not all insurance companies paid for music therapy so I should check with Mia's provider to see if it was covered. I told her that Mia's insurance would soon be cancelled, so it wouldn't matter if they paid for it or not at this point. The next item of discussion was Mia's income, and what she had been doing prior to the stroke. I shared with her that Mia had gone from working as a private duty nurse and earning a decent income to earning nothing. Telling her story was hard, and I couldn't hold back the tears. She was empathetic and told me how music therapy had helped stroke patients walk better and do things they had been told they would never do. It had helped one nurse regain her independence, and she had returned to full-time employment. She also went on to tell me that the center offered scholarships, which was good news. I needed to complete an application and pay the application fee to get the process started. "The sooner you complete it and get it back to us, the sooner Mia can get started," she said. "No worries," I replied. I knew I was in the right place.

OUR GRATITUDE LESSON: New expectations set the groundwork for new choices.

YOUR GRATITUDE LESSON: Describe a time when you expected the best and the best followed.

April 2

Bedtime Stories

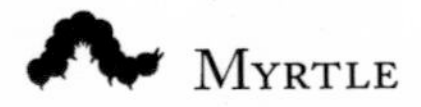 MYRTLE

While Mia was in the hospital, I started reading her bedtime stories and kept it up once we got home. I knew that reading to children boosted brain development and accelerated their mastery of language so I was willing to give it a try. I had nothing to lose.

Tonight the story was about a young woman who had gone through a painful divorce, moved into an apartment, and gone shopping to replace some of the things she had left behind. What she wound up buying was a coffee mug, a pen, and a prayer journal, which helped her put the past behind her and move on with her life. Mia said that the story reminded her of journaling and how she had never stuck with it. She said she was ready to give it another try and asked me what I thought her life would have been like had she stuck with it. I couldn't answer that question and neither could she, but I reminded her that what she could do was use the story to get started and see how things played out. She liked the story and thanked me for sharing it. I thanked the writer.

OUR GRATITUDE LESSON: If history were taught in the form of stories, it would never be forgotten. -Rudyard Kipling

YOUR GRATITUDE LESSON: When was the last time you read a good story that changed the way you felt or inspired you to act on something you've been putting off doing?

April 3

Smart Phones

 Myrtle

We went to the phone store today. I had a new phone and needed to get my data transferred. It was something Mia usually helped me with, so having to go to the store to get it done was yet another sad reminder of how much of Mia's brain had been affected by the stroke, and how much I missed the old Mia. My cousin who worked in the store checked me in and while waiting for my name to be called, Mia asked him if her phone had voice command. He checked and told her that it did, and showed her how to use it. She couldn't wait to get home to test it. She would later discover that voice command would also help her learn to spell and do other things that she had forgotten how to do.

OUR GRATITUDE LESSON: "Thank you God for smart phones, the person that invented them, and a cousin who showed me how to use mine." -Mia

YOUR GRATITUDE LESSON: List five good things that having a smart phone enables you to do.

April 4

A Fanny Pack

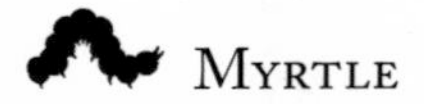 MYRTLE

Before the stroke, Mia wouldn't have been caught anywhere in public with a fanny pack. She called them "old folk's purses." I told her I was going to get me one because carrying anything that weighed over two pounds caused pain in my neck and shoulders. That made me "old folks" but I was okay with it. I was surprised when she asked me to get her one. "Really?" I asked her in disbelief. "Yes," she replied, explaining that she needed it because she could no longer carry her regular purse. An "old folk's purse" was as close to a purse that she could handle, so off we went to find one.

OUR GRATITUDE LESSON: Never say what you won't do. Eating words does not make for a tasty meal.

YOUR GRATITUDE LESSON: List five things in your wallet you would hate to lose? Where would you carry them if you didn't have a wallet?

April 5

Good News

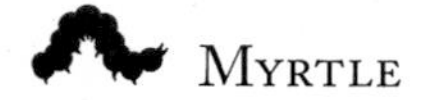 Myrtle

Today we received a letter from the IRS. Mia's tax debt had been placed in "non-collectible" status, so I could check that off my list for now. One rarely gets good news from the IRS. Maybe it had something to do with the change of seasons; it was spring, a time for breakthroughs and renewal. It was time to let go of the sadness and grief. Little blessings were occurring every day, indicators that raised my expectations that more good was on the way. I told Mia about the letter, filed it away, and moved on. Like the seasons that could not be held down, neither would we.

OUR GRATITUDE LESSON: If you can find a way to be thankful for your troubles, like the seasons that change, good has to follow.

YOUR GRATITUDE LESSON: Describe the last piece of good news you received. How did you show gratitude when you received it?

April 9

Gratitude Journaling

MYRTLE

Mia mentioned journaling again, so I suggested that she start with something simple: a gratitude journal. At the end of each day, I asked her to list ten things that she was thankful for. Now that she knew how to use voice activation on her smart phone, she could simply speak the words into the phone and get the correct spelling in a text message. So once again, she began journaling, and again she vowed to stick with it. At the top of the list of things to be grateful for was a delicious home-cooked meal, including dessert, which a cousin brought over. She also gave Mia money. Once again Mia was touched by how loving family could be.

OUR GRATITUDE LESSON: We never run out of second chances. What we usually run out of is time.

YOUR GRATITUDE LESSON: Most regrets expressed by individuals at the end of life are regrets for things they didn't do. List at least three things you feel you must do before you die. Now journal about what's holding you back.

April 13

A Seizure

 MYRTLE

Raymond had volunteered to sit with Mia for the afternoon while I went to work. At around 2:30 p.m. my cell rang; it was him. I could tell by the way he said my name that something was wrong. "Myrtle, this is Raymond. Something is wrong with Mia. Come home. Come on. She's on the floor and I can't get her up. I was in the living room reading and she was in her room and I heard her yell 'Mama' real loud. I got up and went into her room, and she was on the floor." He was short of breath and sounded as if he'd been running. I felt myself getting nervous; my hands trembled. "Is she able to talk?" I asked. He began yelling "Mia, Mia, can you hear me?" I didn't hear her say anything, so I asked him to put the phone up to her ear. I asked her a couple of questions. She just babbled. I couldn't understand a word she said. "Call 911! I'm on the way," I told him. "I already have," he replied. I got up from my desk, grabbed my things, and headed for the door.

I had a sinking feeling when I left the office, thinking she'd had another stroke. When I pulled into the apartment complex I saw a fire truck and noticed two firemen walking around as if they were looking for something. I rolled my window down and asked them who they were looking for, and they gave me our address. I told them to follow me. I rounded the corner and saw an ambulance moving slowly. They, too, were searching for the apartment. I later learned that Raymond had given them the wrong address; he was too nervous to remember.

I parked, got out of the car, and they followed me inside. Mia was lying on the floor. Her eyes were open and she looked confused. Both the firemen and the ambulance attendants assessed the situation. The firemen left, and the ambulance attendants started asking routine questions. Raymond answered what he could, but Mia didn't say anything. I gave them some background information and her medication list. They put her on the stretcher and wheeled her out to the ambulance. As they were connecting her to the equipment in the ambulance, she began to look anxious. I asked her if she knew where she was. She didn't. I asked her if she knew what had happened to her. She didn't. I could tell she was afraid. I explained that we were headed to the hospital to find out what happened to her and that I would be following the ambulance. She nodded, although I don't know whether she really understood.

So there I was trailing an ambulance again…I was jittery, puzzled, afraid, and praying that Mia had not had another stroke. I asked myself what had brought this on. She was so different from how she'd been when I left her at noon. I had picked her up from therapy and stopped to get her a smoothie. We'd talked about how much she enjoyed therapy; how she and the therapist had walked outside, and how proud she was to have taken baby steps without her cane. She was looking forward to the afternoon with her uncle and had already decided what they would eat for lunch. And now this. Mercy.

We arrived at the ER somewhere between 4:00 and 5:00 p.m., and I went to the waiting area to check in. I knew the routine. The receptionist asked me the patient's name and looked it up on the monitor. She then looked up at me and asked, "Did you say the patient's name was Mia Russell?" "Yes, I replied. "Is she a nurse?" she asked. I answered yes, fighting back tears. "Did she ever work in Humboldt?" "Yes, she worked at a rehab center." I knew where this was headed, so I went ahead and told her about Mia's stroke in January. "Oh my God," she said, as she got up and came around the counter with outstretched arms. "I know Mia. She took care of my mother when she was in the rehab center. My mother just loved her and I loved her and I am so sorry to hear this. She was such a good, caring nurse. Oh my God. No." At this point tears were flowing down my face. We held each other for a few seconds and then she went back behind the desk. "You are not going to sit out here. You need to be with your daughter, so just give me a minute and I'll find her and get you back there," she said.

She checked her monitor again, made a call, then wrote my name on a green sticker and placed it on my jacket. "They are taking her to a room now. Do you mind if I take you to Mia?" she asked. "I want to see her and let her know that I will be praying for her." I nodded and we headed back to where Mia was. When we got there, they were connecting her to equipment. The receptionist went to the right side of the bed and I stood at the left. She explained to Mia who she was and why she wanted to see her. She could see the confusion on Mia's face but that didn't seem to matter to her.

She just wanted to see her and let her know that she would be praying for her recovery. She hugged me again and left. It was good to know Mia had done good work in the past. It would pay off in more ways that we could even imagine that night in the ER.

Shortly after the receptionist left, Mia started to talk. Her speech was better this time. She was beginning to remember what happened to her. "I was in my…wheelchair. I saw…lights flashing…real bright. I was shaking. My chair…turned over. Next thing...I'm on…floor and called… your … name….real…loud. I was so scared…Mama." As she was describing what happened, it came to me, that she'd had a seizure. A CT scan confirmed it, and she was admitted to the neurology floor for observation. Thank God it wasn't another stroke.

She got to a room around 9:30 p.m. that night and of course next came blood work, unnecessary pokes and sticks to her tiny veins by phlebotomists who blamed their inability to hit her veins on everything except the truth: they just didn't have the skills. No one knew that better than Mia, since she had worked in phlebotomy for a few years, in a pediatric lab where small veins were the norm, and she mastered it. She knew that a skilled technician would likely hit the vein on the first stick. At first she was patient with the phlebotomists, but she knew when to tell them to stop poking and find someone with experience. Finally, a nurse started the IV and loaded Mia up with seizure medication. She had a restful night.

OUR GRATITUDE LESSON: Never would I have imagined being thankful for a seizure, but tonight was different. As I sat at her bedside and dozed, my worst fears had been laid to rest; she had not had another stroke.

YOUR GRATITUDE STORY: Usually our problems stem from thinking about something that happened in the past or something that is going to happen in the future. Describe a time when you thought the worst but the worst never happened?

April 14

Something to Sing About

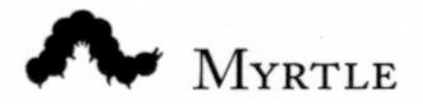

MYRTLE

The neurologist came in this morning with good news –Mia could go home. He changed her seizure medication and told us that it was okay for her to resume therapy. Raymond showed up just in time to help us get packed up and we headed home.

There was a song playing on the car radio. I don't remember what song it was but Mia started singing. Even though she sang out of tune, it sounded good to my ears. This was another little milestone. Usually when we get in the car she holds her head down to prevent motion sickness. Today was different. She sang with joy. I chimed in and we sang all the way home, occasionally glancing at each other and smiling. Later she told me that she was just happy that her stay in the hospital was short and that Cameron was headed home to spend the weekend with her. It was going to be a great weekend!

Cameron made it home safely and got busy as soon as he arrived. He washed Mia's vehicle and aired up the tires; something she'd wanted done because it hadn't been driven since she had the stroke. My plate was full, so I hadn't had time to deal with it. After Cameron finished the vehicle, they looked at language apps her speech therapist had suggested, and he purchased a couple of them and got them loaded onto her iPad. She showed him what she was working on in physical therapy and was proud to get a "thumbs up" from her big brother.

I cooked a big meal, mostly their favorite foods, and we enjoyed the weekend. It was short but meaningful. On Sunday around noon I packed up leftovers for Cameron, and he headed back to Chattanooga. He left Mia with an exercise prescription, exercise bands, and as always, encouraging words. With a big smile on her face, she sat in her wheelchair and watched through the window as he pulled away. I went upstairs where she wouldn't see me cry. Even though it had been a good weekend, I felt sad and alone. I wished he lived closer. I wished there was someone who really understood what I was going through and could speak some words to me that would make these sad feelings go away. But I knew I was wishing for the impossible. I had to ride it out, and feel the pain, so I let the cleansing tears flow.

After a good cry, gratitude showed up and reminded me that I still had a lot to be thankful for. I had a good son who loved his sister, and I remembered what he said after washing her vehicle. He said he washed it because he believed that she would drive again. He believed she would regain her independence, and we would get through it together. I held on to those thoughts and moved on with my day. Mia was in a happy place and that was enough.

OUR GRATITUDE LESSON: Most often, the tears shed at gravesites are for words that were not said and deeds that were not done.

YOUR GRATITUDE STORY: List five good things that you have to sing about? Were they things that you did for someone else or things that were done for you?

April 21

Birds On The Line

 MYRTLE

Today two amazing things happened. The first one happened on the way to therapy. We were driving down the street and Mia noticed what she called two owls perched on the power lines. When she asked me if I saw them I wanted to stop the car to look, but there were cars behind me. So I looked in the rearview mirror and did see two birds, not owls. What's amazing about seeing birds on a power line? In order for Mia to see the birds she had to look to her right side and looking to the right was something she had to be reminded to do since she had the stroke. Today she decided to look on her own. Did this mean that new things were happening with her brain, new pathways being created? I wasn't sure, but what I was sure of was that this was another milestone, another special moment, a new gratitude entry.

"I can't believe…I see that. You know… on that…side. I saw… it… Mama. I'm getting…better." she said, grinning. "I.. got… to…call…my brother." She immediately whipped out her phone and shared her good news. I guess she forgot that looking down at the phone while the car was moving usually caused her to get dizzy and nauseated. This time it didn't. More progress.

When I picked her up from therapy, she had more good news to share. For the first time, with assistance from the physical therapist, she had taken a few steps with a regular cane. She was thrilled and so was I.

OUR GRATITUDE LESSON: Seeing is believing.

YOUR GRATITUDE STORY: List five milestones in your life, big or small.

April 22

Closed Doors and Opened Windows

 Myrtle

I got the inevitable call from Mia's job today. FMLA was ending, and her insurance would be terminated at the end of the month. The representative told me I would get the termination notice via Fed Ex. It arrived two days later. She also informed me that she would be sending me information on COBRA coverage, which might be an option until Mia could return to work. A COBRA plan would cost $860/month which was not even an option. I ended the call on that note, grateful for the services her insurance had provided. I returned to faith and prayer, thankful in advance that things would fall into place at the right time.

A few minutes after hanging up with Mia's employer, April called to say that she and Carla wanted to come and stay with Mia a couple of days a week so I could get back to work at least part time. Three days later I received a call that Mia's Social Security Disability application had been approved. One door had closed, but two windows had opened.

OUR GRATITUDE LESSON: Without faith, nothing is possible. With it, nothing is impossible. -Mary McLeod Bethune

YOUR GRATITUDE STORY: Describe a time when you acted on faith and it turned out to be a major turning point in your life.

May 6

Supplemental Security Income

MYRTLE

Mia received her first Supplemental Security Income (SSI) check. Because she'd had short term disability insurance on her job, she didn't qualify for the full SSI benefit, but every little bit helped. It's a good thing to live in a country that offers financial assistance to the needy. Qualifying for SSI meant she automatically qualified for Medicaid. Two blessings. To go from earning $3,500 a month to an income of $490 a month may not be anything to brag about, but it was better than nothing. We would accept the check with gratitude and hold fast to believing that things would keep getting better.

OUR GRATITUDE LESSON: Sometimes when everything seems to be going wrong, be still. Behind the scenes they may actually be going right.

YOUR GRATITUDE STORY: More things are accomplished by prayer than the world realizes. List five prayers you've had answered.

May 7

Good Grief!

 MYRTLE

We took our first trip out of town; we went to Nashville to one of Mia's favorite places to shop. I thought it would be good for her, cheer her up a bit. My godson went with us. We bought a few things, ate at our favorite restaurant, and made it back home safely. Mia said she enjoyed the trip, and I thought all was well. But later that night when I went into her room to read to her and say goodnight, she started to cry. It was the first time I had seen her cry since the stroke.

When I asked her why she was crying, she opened up about how she felt. She told me that she was sad because I bought shoes for myself at the mall and she couldn't buy any. She loved shoes and always looked forward to summer when she could wear cute sandals. But the stroke had left her with foot drop and that meant she was not able to keep a sandal on her left foot. She said life wasn't fair. She talked about how uncomfortable she was in the restaurant because she was afraid that people would be staring at her if she had food around her mouth while she was eating. She didn't like using the bathroom because she needed help, and she knew she was slowing me down by asking me to help her. She liked to drive and always drove on long trips, but this time she couldn't. She knew I didn't like city driving and always took a nap, but now I had to do all the driving, and it wasn't fair to me. And then she just bawled. It was heartbreaking for both of us.

I hadn't given any thought to any of her concerns related to the trip. I thought I had prepared myself mentally, and when I mentioned going she was all smiles, so to sit there and watch her cry wasn't easy. I did my best to comfort her, held her as she cried, and said a silent prayer that peace would follow the sadness. I knew that stroke patients or anyone who has suffered loss experience periods of sadness. I realized that the shoe store and almost everything we did that day must have in some way reminded her of her loss. It didn't matter if the loss was temporary or permanent; for her it was loss, and she was sad about it and it would take time to work through it. I stayed with her until she stopped crying. She wanted to talk to her brother, so she made the call and felt better after talking to him.

OUR GRATITUDE LESSON: Wear your grief like a warm sweater, until the cold chill passes.

YOUR GRATITUDE STORY: We all experience grief but we don't all express it in the same way. Want to express it in a healthy way? Write about it.

May 12

Baby Steps

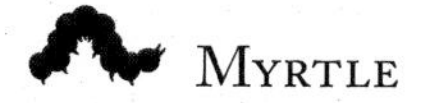

Myrtle

It is Mother's Day weekend, which meant Mia would get to spend another weekend with her brother. She couldn't wait to show him how she could take a few steps without her cane. Shortly after he arrived on Friday evening, while sitting in the living room, she strapped on her helmet, pushed her wheelchair back out of the way, and stood up from her favorite seat on the couch. Like a baby walking for the first time, she balanced herself for a few seconds and slowly, but confidently, took about 10 steps. Cameron's mouth flew open. For just a few seconds he was speechless. Then he told us that on his walk from his truck, he wondered what progress she had made since his last visit two weeks earlier. He had expected progress but hadn't imagined her walking. He looked at her and gave her that pleasing grin, the kind a coach gives his players when they have beaten the odds. She proudly sat back down, removed her helmet, and looked at me with that innocent but confident little-girl smile. Had she been able to wink, I think she would have.

I remembered my mother's words whenever we complained that we couldn't do something: "You can do anything you want to do if you put your mind to it." Mia's mind was on walking again. She reminded me of the track and field sprinter, Wilma Rudolph. Wilma had been a sickly child who was diagnosed with double pneumonia, scarlet fever, and polio. She was told that she would never walk again. Her mother refused to accept the diagnosis and committed herself to working with her daughter to overcome her challenges. As for Wilma, here's what she had to say about it: "My doctor told me I would never walk again. My mother told me I would. I believed my mother." Not only did Wilma overcome her disabilities, she went on to break world records in track and field at the 1960 Olympics in Rome. Mia was determined to walk again, and today she took a few steps to prove it.

OUR GRATITUDE LESSON: Most people don't fail, they give up trying.

YOUR GRATITUDE STORY: List five things you've accomplished over the last ten years.

May 14

Mothers

 MYRTLE

This Mother's Day took on new meaning for me, thanks partly to Mia and to memories of my mother. Mama had several of what we children called "old folks" sayings that often fell on deaf ears and inattentive minds when we were growing up. Although she died in 2004, on January 9th when I found Mia lying on the bedroom floor and couldn't remember where my phone was, it was my mother's spirit that said to me "Be still and get a hold of yourself" (one of her often repeated sayings) so you'll know what to do. Often sitting at Mia's bedside in the hospital, sometimes around the clock, I could hear Mama saying, "A man works from sun to sun, but a mother's work is never done." Now I understood exactly what she meant.

It doesn't matter who you are or what your station in life happens to be, you ought to have something good to say about your mother. After all, there's not a person on this earth who did not pass through the womb of a woman, thereby making her a mother. Life flows from mothers. For anyone who doesn't believe it, "keep living;" this was another one of my mother's sayings. If you live long enough, as sure as the sun rises in the east and sets in the west, you'll come to realize the role God gave mothers.

I fully accepted that I would not be where I am in life without my mother. I realized how much I had to be thankful for. I was grateful that the seeds of good she planted decades ago were still growing through the love shown toward her granddaughter. I was happy that my son took the time to spend this Mother's Day with me and Mia. And I was grateful that whenever I was feeling down, Mama's spirit reminded me that God would get me through it. It was a good day.

OUR GRATITUDE LESSON: No gift to your mother can ever equal the gift she gives to you: Life.

YOUR GRATITUDE STORY: List five reasons you are thankful for your mother.

May 16

Medicaid

MYRTLE

There was a gap between the time Mia's private insurance was cancelled and the start of Medicaid so I was relieved and grateful to receive her Medicaid pharmacy card in the mail today; I thought about all the people whose health had deteriorated because they couldn't pay for medication and didn't know where to turn for assistance. I thought of those who lived in countries where there was no Medicaid. I thought about how I had complained about having to wait in long pharmacy lines when I picked up medication, and how the next time I picked it up I wouldn't have to pay for it. I decided to change my attitude and stop complaining.

OUR GRATITUDE LESSON: If we thought more, we would thank more.

YOUR GRATITUDE STORY: If you have health insurance, list five reasons you're grateful to have it.

May 20

Bonds

 MYRTLE

We were invited to Cousin Jeremy's 50th birthday party, and Mia was excited. Jeremy was a technician in rehab at the hospital, and when he heard about Mia's stroke he came to the neurology floor to visit her and check on me. Prior to her hospital stay, Mia and Jeremy barely knew each other, but their grandparents were brother and sister and their dads had been best friends and graduated from high school together. There was a bond that at the time Mia knew nothing of.

Once she was transferred to the rehab unit, Jeremy began working with her and based on their interactions with each other, it seemed as if they had known each other all their lives. Jeremy had a great sense of humor, and since the stroke Mia had verbalized exactly what she thought, so right away they clashed, but they also clicked. Even on days when he was not assigned to take care of her, he would come into her room like a drill sergeant, demanding that she get up and get busy. Each time he did it, she fired back, telling him to get out of her room because he was not her tech, and not to come back. He in turn would leave laughing or sometimes looking bewildered. Nonetheless, he made it his business to check on her every day, and on the days he was off, she asked about him and mentioned how she missed him bugging her. So when he called to ask for our mailing address so he could send us an invitation to his birthday party, Mia was excited and said she definitely wanted to attend.

We went to the party and had a good time. It was good to see people I hadn't seen in a while. The highlight for Mia was the pictures she took with Jeremy, which she still keeps on a table in her bedroom.

OUR GRATITUDE LESSON: The bonds of love connect us, even to the third generation.

YOUR GRATITUDE STORY: List five people with whom you have a strong bond. When you're finished, write them a note or give them a call to tell them how you feel about them.

May 25

Anger

 MYRTLE

Anger is a stage of grieving, and grieving is about loss. For the first time since January 9th, I felt loss, and I was angry. I wanted my old life back and wanted Mia to have hers. It was a Thursday evening. I had worked all day, come home, helped Mia with her bath, and needed to run errands. She was going with me but moving slowly, so I yelled at her to speed up. I could tell that I had hurt her feelings, but at the time I just wanted to get going. While we were out, she started crying, and not thinking, I asked her what was wrong? "I feel sad…when…you…upset" she said. "I know …I slow… you down and you don't like…that." She was exactly right, I thought to myself. I'm a task oriented, get it done type of person and because of the stroke, she was now a slow poke.

I was angry that I couldn't just jump into the car and run errands the way I used to. I was angry at being a caregiver; it was not the future I had imagined. I was also angry because Mia's stroke had put a financial burden on me that I had not anticipated. And I was sad because regardless of whether her disabilities were temporary or permanent, the daughter, the friend I had come to laugh and have fun with, was no longer there. Sad because it felt as if a piece of me was slowly dying. Sad because in 2013 I had moved in with her to help her get back on track after an ugly divorce, and she had made so much progress and was so proud of herself, only to have this happen. Yes, I was visibly upset.

Although I wasn't calling it that at the time, I was also grieving. Just as individuals who are chronically and terminally ill experience grief, so do caregivers. When grief isn't properly addressed on the front end it can cause depression, feelings of hopelessness, or negatively impact your health in other ways. I knew all of that, and I knew I had to do something constructive to get through this bad time. So I turned to what I always turn to in a crisis: my journal. I had to get these feelings of anger out of my head and heart and I knew that putting them on paper was the best way to do it.

Not only did journaling help me feel better but it also led me to possible solutions to help Mia cope with her grief. I knew she was suffering in ways I could not imagine. In addition to her listing things she was grateful for in her journal, I began making prayer cards for her which were really affirmations, and I asked her to rewrite them. She liked the idea and wanted me to tape the cards up in her bathroom and bedroom as daily reminders. I did.

Crocheting had been Mia's favorite hobby, but with no use of her right hand, that was out. We talked about her finding something else that she could enjoy and decided to add it to our gratitude journals; we would thank God in advance for a new hobby. Answers came quickly. It turned out to be "word search" and Sudoku. Not only did they give her something to do to pass the time, but research shows that they help develop more complex connections among brain cells, thereby helping the brain compensate for the loss of cells caused by the stroke. So we set out to find "word search" activity books, and I never realized there were so many themes to choose from. She also mentioned she had done Sudoku before and asked for the Sudoku page from the local newspaper. She began working them as well. Although she frequently complained about how hard they were to solve, she stuck with it and in time would learn that hobbies do more than chase the blues away.

This wouldn't be our last confrontation with anger and I certainly don't claim to have mastered it, but I'm grateful I knew that if we didn't deal with it, it would deal with us, and the outcome would not be pretty.

OUR GRATITUDE LESSON: Anger is one letter away from danger!

YOUR GRATITUDE STORY: When is the last time you've been angry about something? Did it cause you to hurt someone's feelings? If so, did you apologize?

May 31

A Gratitude Story

 MYRTLE

I read Mia a story about a graduate who had to give a graduation speech and decided that instead of giving the traditional speech, she would use the opportunity to say "thank you" to the people who had made a difference in her life. She shared with the audience that when she was growing up, her mother always spoke of the importance of writing "thank you" notes, and even though at the time she hated the idea, she had grown to learn that her mother was right. So that night, she pulled out her "thank you" notes, and graciously expressed her appreciation to her parents, teachers, friends, staff, and administrators for their contributions to her school success.

What a novel idea! There is absolutely nothing that matches what you feel when you express gratitude. When I finished the story, Mia said she compared it to the idea of sending "thank you" cards to the people who had been so nice to us. Although her gratitude journey had just begun, I could see subtle positive changes in her attitude. The story left us both yearning for the opportunity to do something similar and I believed that the time to do it would soon come.

OUR GRATITUDE LESSON: Thank God that kindness and gratitude will always be best friends.

YOUR GRATITUDE STORY: List your five favorite teachers. What made them different? Have you expressed your gratitude to them? If not, why not now? Even if they have died, still write them a thank you note in your journal.

June 2

Anticipation

MYRTLE

Mia was scheduled to have the missing piece of her skull replaced on June 19th, so after therapy we stopped by the hospital for her to do her pre-admission screening. The missing piece, called the flap, had been stored in a lab in the hospital's basement for more than five months, and she was eager to get it back where it belonged, on her head. She had mentioned several times how she was ready to get back to a comfortable sleeping position. She was also tired of looking at the dent in the left side of her head that had become quite noticeable. And even though she was grateful for the protection her helmet provided, she was tired of wearing it, tired of the stares from people when she was in public. For her, June 19th wouldn't come soon enough.

OUR GRATITUDE LESSON: Pleasure and trouble are both greatest in anticipation.

YOUR GRATITUDE STORY: What part of your body do you treasure the most? What would life be like without it?

June 3

A Good Barber

 Myrtle

Mia wanted to get a haircut before the surgery and her brother wouldn't be back in town until the day of the surgery, so I recommended my barber. She wasn't too excited about the idea. Cameron knew how to cut her hair and how to be careful cutting around the incision site so that it didn't hurt. She didn't think that my barber would be able to do that. I reminded her that he had been cutting hair for over 30 years and he could do it because he was a good barber. I told her that the biggest challenge would be getting in and out of the shop, not him cutting her hair. She fired back that it was easy for me to say but reluctantly agreed to give him a try.

When we arrived at the shop, my barber came out to help Mia up the steps and into his shop. She appreciated his help; things were off to a good start. Once we got inside, he helped her to the chair, draped her, looked closely at her head and the scar from the incision, and asked her how she wanted it cut. He didn't appear to be a bit apprehensive. When he finished, he handed her the mirror. She looked at me and smiled and said "good job." It was then that he shared with us that he was a little nervous when he walked out to the car and saw the helmet. "That helmet scared me. I didn't know what to expect, but I couldn't let you'll know that," he admitted. We all laughed. Mia thanked him, gave him a tip, and he helped her back to the car. When we drove off, she took another look in the mirror and said she was going to call her brother and tell him that my barber had him beat, and that it didn't take him nearly as long to get the job done. Of course she did just that and we all had another good laugh.

OUR GRATITUDE LESSON: A little "heart work" makes any job easier.

YOUR GRATITUDE STORY: Almost everyone has sat in the chair of a barber or stylist. List three things you like about yours.

June 6

The Healing Power of Music

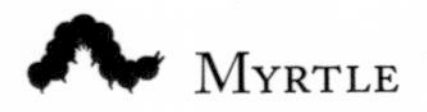

Myrtle

Mia had her first music session. She liked it and couldn't wait to tell me about it when I picked her up. She told me how the therapist had her walking to the beat of music and when she asked her why, she was told that when she walked to the beat of the music, she didn't drag her weak foot. Mia called her "sneaky," and they both laughed. Their relationship was off to a good start.

Like the other therapists, nurses, and hospital technicians who had worked with Mia, the music therapist immediately recognized her candid sense of humor. "Seems like everywhere I go since I had the stroke, people tell me I am funny and they like me Mama," Mia told me after her session. "That's because you're special," I told her. This was a new Mia. Mia before the stroke was best described as bossy, direct, and a take charge kind of person, but she was not known for being humorous, and her bossiness was sometimes unwelcome. The stroke had changed her and we both knew it.

The therapist worked on teaching Mia her phone number and address. Mia couldn't believe that she was actually learning it while listening to music. She left the session feeling like the therapist really knew what she was doing. After all, she knew a little about music herself and shared that with her therapist. She had taken piano lessons from ages 5 to 14.

I was convinced that music would make a big impact on Mia's progress. I'd read stories of how it had helped stroke and Alzheimer's patients regain memory loss. How it had brought smiles to the faces of children battling terminal illness. Music is a gift from God, a healing medicine for the mind, body, and soul, and it was going to work its magic on Mia.

OUR GRATITUDE LESSON: Music washes away from the soul the dust of everyday life. -Berthold Auerbach

YOUR GRATITUDE STORY: List three ways music improves your mood or makes life better.

June 9

Godmothers

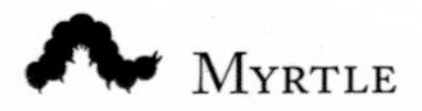

MYRTLE

April and I were often told that we looked alike. When we heard that, we would say it was because our mothers were sisters. I never gave it much thought until one day an acquaintance of April's spotted me from a distance and yelled out "April!" Not knowing who he was, I ignored him. He then got out of the car and yelled, "Why are you pretending that you don't know who I am?" As he got closer, I saw that he looked a little tipsy. "I'm not April, I'm her cousin," I said to him. He blinked hard a couple of times and apologized. I couldn't help but laugh. He got back in the car, gave me another hard stare, and motioned to the driver to get going.

For years when Mia and I ran into April, she jokingly referred to Mia as her second daughter and Mia called April her second mother. Never would we have imagined that those casual words exchanged in passing would someday be taken literally.

In 2016 at a family reunion (before Mia's stroke), April got sick just before time to board the bus and head for home. I was headed to the restaurant and heard about it and went back to the room to tell Mia. She was still in bed but immediately jumped up, slipped on some clothes and we headed to April's room. We met her and family members in the hallway just outside her door; they were struggling to try to get her to the elevator. April couldn't stand up. Her legs looked rubbery and her feet were dragging; it didn't look good. Mia and I looked at her, looked at each other, and told the family that we needed to get her back to the room. There was no way they were going to make it to the bus with her in that condition.

We turned her around and made it back inside the door, where she flopped down on the bed. She was sweating profusely but coherent. We asked her a few questions and learned that she had been vomiting and that this was not her first episode. She had taken medication for it but it wasn't working, partly because she was throwing it back up. Mia and I decided what needed to be done to get the medication to work and Mia took charge. Our plan worked, and after a few minutes she settled down and regained her strength. We found a wheelchair and got her to the bus, where family was waiting. They made it two hours down the interstate and she had another sick spell. The bus driver got her to the nearest hospital and she was admitted.

Later in the afternoon when Mia and I were driving home, we stopped at the hospital to check on April. She was back to normal and thanked her "second daughter" for saving her life, saying she could never repay her for what she had done. Mia told her that she did what any nurse would have done in a similar situation: she didn't panic and simply used the skills she had learned.

Six months later and the roles are reversed. April had become a "second mother" to Mia, and things were going unbelievably well. Aside from looking alike, they were surprised to discover that they had a few other things in common. They liked some of the same television shows, had similar taste in shoes, and they slept a lot. As things continued to unfold, there was no question in our minds that April was a God-send, a godmother to her "second daughter." It had to be God, what I call the spirit of good, working behind the scenes because I could not pay April what she deserved for sitting with Mia, yet she came faithfully whenever I needed her. When she couldn't come, Cousin Carla came. They were loyal, and loyalty would soon have its rewards.

Mia was fortunate to have three godmothers. The second is Cousin Gwen who has always been an anchor for Mia and for me. She's a good cook and Mia loves her desserts. Since the stroke she has baked Mia's favorites and made special trips to deliver them since she doesn't live in the same city. She and her family have hosted dinners and been most accommodating. She consistently sent Mia inspirational cards after the surgery, along with cash to help with Mia's personal expenses. God always sends the right people at the right time.

Her third godmother is Helen, a friend I met when I moved to Wisconsin in the early 1970s; a nurturing person who was like the big sister I never had. When Cameron was born she invited me to her home, where we stayed for a week while she took care of us. We left Wisconsin a year later; the winters were torturous. Even though we were separated by hundreds of miles, Helen has been a mainstay in Cameron and Mia's lives; she has been present for every major milestone including Mia's recovery.

When I called to let her know that Mia had had the stroke, she offered to come and stay for a while to give me a break. I asked her to wait until later so when she did make the trip, even though it was a short visit, the three of us enjoyed the time spent together. It was a visit Mia says she will never forget.

These three women are testaments to the true meaning of the term "godmother." It has nothing to do with christenings or rituals or my choosing them to be in involved in Mia's life if something happened to me. They were not asked to do anything; they simply showed up, got involved, and made a difference.

OUR GRATITUDE LESSON: Mothers can't be everywhere and do everything, so God sent godmothers. I am blessed to have three! -Mia

YOUR GRATITUDE STORY: Everybody has a godmother story. Write about yours. Whether she is living or not, don't forget to thank her.

June 11

Nostalgia

 MYRTLE

Cousin Amy stopped by this morning to drop off a bag of Georgia peaches. What's so special about Georgia peaches you ask? These peaches remind me of my childhood summers.

Anyone who knows me well enough knows how much I appreciate good home-grown, home-cooked fruits and vegetables. Amy knows me. My paternal grandparents always had a garden, and we ate something from the garden every single day that I stayed in their home. My mother and a few of my aunts were excellent cooks and because of them and my grandparents, there are still a few nostalgic tastes that I crave. Peaches are one of them.

I used to get excited when I saw peaches at the grocery store or at roadside stands that looked and smelled good. I'd buy them, only to be disappointed when I got home and bit into one. They were either too mushy or too hard and almost never sweet. Each summer I hoped for something better. Each summer they got worse until I finally gave up. So when Amy called to say that she was going to be coming to visit and bringing Georgia peaches, I got excited. This time I got my wish. They were the sweetest, juiciest peaches I'd eaten in years, the kind that when you bit into it, the juice trickled down your chin and elbow and it didn't matter. Growing up I remember peddlers driving through the neighborhood with bushels of them on the backs of their trucks. Mama always bought enough to make cobblers, fried pies, and preserves for the winter.

The peaches that Amy bought were so good that I had to share them, although I could have easily eaten them all myself. Mia wasn't a big peach fan but said they were the best she had ever tasted. "Sweet and juicy" is how she described them. I shared them with a couple of co-workers who knew good fruit when they tasted it. Of course they wanted more but there were no more to be had.

OUR GRATITUDE LESSON: Good fruit is a nutritious gift from the sky, the earth, laborious hands, and in my case, a thoughtful friend and cousin who knew me well.

YOUR GRATITUDE STORY: What were your favorite childhood foods? How many of them do you still enjoy?

June 12

Two Brains

 Myrtle

At 7:00 a.m. I went in to give Mia her medicine, hoping she would remember that today was her birthday. She didn't. She had no recollection of important dates and events. She couldn't remember the days of the week or the months, so when I reminded her that today was her birthday, her first question was, "So how old am I?" "Thirty-eight," I replied. "Is that old," she asked? "I know... I'm not ...old as you...but I don't know what thirty-eight means." Holding back tears, I did my best to explain, knowing all too well that my explanation wouldn't fix her memory and that she would need constant reminders for a very long time.

Most of the cells in our body are replaced over a period of time but when strokes occur, brain cells or neurons, are destroyed and not replaced. For the most part, we are born with all the neurons we will ever need, an estimated one hundred billion to one trillion. In Mia's case, the attack was on the left side of her brain, which is the language and communication center. One of the unique things about the human brain is its two hemispheres, referred to by some scientists as two brains. Under normal circumstances the two brains complement each other, sort of like having two kidneys. When one is damaged, the second one kicks in to help the individual function as normally as possible. In Mia's case she had forgotten her birthday because every day was the same to her. However, I'd begun to notice that she was becoming more intuitive and more open to change and new possibilities. Before the stroke she was rigid and somewhat of a perfectionist. But now she was friendlier and funnier and more expressive regardless of the environment. There was a definite change in her personality, all of which I attributed to her right brain kicking in and compensating for the damage caused by the left.

So she ended the day with something new to add to her gratitude journal; she had learned that she had two brains to help her get better and regain her independence. She was determined that she wanted to make the best of the good neurons she had he left. Repetition of tasks is what makes neuroplasticity successful and I was determined to continue searching for activities to keep her engaged. I hoped that by June 12, 2019 she would not only remember her birthday, but also how old she was.

OUR GRATITUDE LESSON: Birthdates are important - only if you can remember them.

YOUR GRATITUDE STORY: List five ways that your life would change if suddenly your brain stopped working properly.

June 17

Uncles

 MYRTLE

Today Mia talked about her uncles and wanted to know how many she had. She knew them all by name but couldn't count them. This was another example of the damage to her left brain, and how the right brain was working to compensate. We had never before had a conversation like this one about her uncles.

I told her that she had 12 uncles living and three who had passed on. "Oh," she remarked with a chuckle. "I knew I had a lot." She went on to talk about how good they had been to her since the stroke, starting with her Uncle Bill who years back had hired her as a photographer for his newspaper and how much she liked taking pictures for him. Bill had been the uncle who never winced when she needed to be put in her place, but he was also one to show up when she needed him, like the time she fell on her bike and he was the first to show up and get her to the doctor. She remembered how her Uncle Dwight used to take her to one of his favorite restaurants and how much the two of them enjoyed eating biscuits there. She talked about how grateful she was that my brothers had been like father figures to her, always looking out for her when she was a little girl. She was just blown away by the fact that her Uncle Timmy had flown in from New York and her Uncle Waymond had driven from Wisconsin to see her when she was in the hospital. How her Uncle Raymond was always in and out to check on us because it was his nature to check on family. She remembered his Valentine's Day throw and pillow, a pillow she has slept on every single night since February 14, 2017. She mentioned her father's brothers and how they looked out for her during her summer visits with her grandparents. They took her and her brothers for rides in her grandfather's "big Buick" and bought them special treats. She remembered spending time with her Uncle "Junior" and his wife during the summer of 2016, and how nice it was to be around them and how much we all looked alike and shared a great sense of humor.

Talking about how good it felt to have so many good uncles was another testament to two things: gratitude journaling, and the fact that the stroke had not destroyed everything. To be honest, these memories were continuing to open her eyes to things to which she had never before given much thought.

OUR GRATITUDE LESSON: I'm as lucky as I can be. The world's best uncles belong to me.

YOUR GRATITUDE STORY: What uncle has made a difference in your life? When's the last time you thanked him?

June 18

Disappointment

MYRTLE

Mia is scheduled to have her skull flap replaced tomorrow, and Cameron had come home to be with us. "As long as my family is there when I go into surgery, I will be alright," she told us when the doctor set the date.

We had just finished dinner when the phone rang. It was the surgeon's nurse calling to say that the surgeon was ill and Mia's surgery would have to be rescheduled. "He thinks it's just a bug that will pass in a couple of days," she said. "So we will let you know as soon as he is back to work so that we can reschedule." I answered with a quiet "thank you," as I turned toward Mia and Cameron, who were both giving me that "oh no, here we go" look.

It was a big disappointment. "Man, I'm tired of not being able to find a good sleeping position. I got myself all ready for this so how can he be sick?" she asked, looking at me as if I had something to do with it. I searched for words to make her feel better, and finally came up with: "You wouldn't want a sick doctor with unsteady hands fooling around with your brain would you?" She shook her head. "So let's just say a prayer that he gets better and gets back to work. Do you think he wants to be sick? And besides, you've waited this long so a few more days won't kill you. You've made it through worse, remember? Let's just be grateful that you have a good surgeon who obviously takes pride in his work. Think about it, he could have just passed you off to another surgeon and I don't think you would've wanted that either." She looked up and said, with a smirk, "Yeah, you're right...but man." Cameron wasn't thrilled either, since he had rearranged his work schedule to be here, but he, too, had to accept it for what it was; it was beyond our control. He spent the day with his sister while I went to work on Monday, which meant they had another opportunity to spend quality time together. We added the surgeon to our gratitude list, thanking God in advance for his full recovery.

OUR GRATITUDE LESSON: An attitude of gratitude can turn the unexpected into perfect timing.

YOUR GRATITUDE STORY: What has been one of your greatest disappointments? What lesson did you learn from it?

June 22

A Regular Cane

 Mia

Today my therapist told me it was time to start using a regular cane. I couldn't wait to tell mama when she came to pick me up. I had been looking at canes when we were out shopping so I asked Mama to take me to get one. When we got to the store I got a mobile shopping cart and went straight to the cane rack and grabbed the one I liked. After Mama paid for it, I took the cart back and asked her to take the tag off the new cane. Then I stood up and walked out the store with a big smile on my face. I looked at Mama, and she was smiling too. I was proud of myself.

OUR GRATITUDE LESSON: I expected to walk again. I'm walking. I'm thankful.

YOUR GRATITUDE STORY: Write about one of your proudest moments.

June 29

Loyalty

 Myrtle

After three months of waiting, April was officially approved to help care for Mia and be paid through the CHOICES Program. This was another prayer answered. Up to now she had volunteered. Getting compensated was icing on the cake. We were all in a happy place.

OUR GRATITUDE LESSON: Loyalty has its rewards.

YOUR GRATITUDE STORY: On a scale of 1–10, how loyal are you? Do you make promises that you don't keep? Write about a time when you were loyal and it paid off.

July 2

It Takes Two

 Mia

Mama hurt her neck in a car wreck several years ago, and so lifting anything heavy makes her neck hurt. This meant that grocery shopping was difficult for her, but thanks to mobile shopping carts and my strong left arm, she didn't have to worry about that now. When we went to the grocery store, I drove the cart and did the heavy lifting. When we got ready to check out, I would put the items on the counter. When we got home, I took them out of the trunk of the car and placed them in her little rolling cart. She rolled it into the house. I also helped take them out of the cart and helped put them away.

OUR GRATITUDE LESSON: I don't see my weakness as a curse. My strong left hand and Mama's right are a perfect match.

YOUR GRATITUDE STORY: Who is the one person you can always count on? When was the last time you expressed your appreciation to that person?

July 7

The Surgeon's Recovery

 MYRTLE

Today I got the call that the surgeon had returned to work, and Mia's surgery was rescheduled for July 12. She was excited when I shared the good news with her and she immediately texted the date to her brothers and April. She was more than ready to get this show on the road.

OUR GRATITUDE LESSON: Blessings; you can't count just one.

YOUR GRATITUDE STORY: List five people you pray for.

July 8

Brownies

 MIA

My Uncle Dwight loves sweets, and he thought I made good brownies. Mama told me that today was his birthday, so I wanted to surprise him with some of my brownies. I asked Mama if she would help me make them, and she said yes. When we finished, she called him and told him to come by to get them on his lunch break. He came by, tasted one and looked at me and said: "See, I told you when you were in the hospital you didn't need two hands to make brownies." I replied: "Yes I did, but one of them was Mama's." He grinned, took his brownies, thanked me, and left.

OUR GRATITUDE LESSON: I felt good making brownies for my uncle. If you want to feel good, do good.

YOUR GRATITUDE STORY: What compliments do you receive on a regular basis? List them in your journal and beside each one, write the words "thank you."

July 12

Getting Her Hard-Head Back

 Myrtle

We arrived at the hospital at 9:00 a.m. Mia got checked in and prepped for surgery. The nurses did what they routinely do in pre-operative care, and the anesthesiologist came in to assess and reassure Mia that everything would be just fine. To ease her mind he asked her about her favorite foods. She told him and then asked him about his favorites. They exchanged a few more words and I'm not sure what Mia said but whatever it was, he started laughing, looked at me and said, "She is going to be just fine." Just before leaving the room he told her to think about her favorite meal when she got to the operating room and when she woke up, perhaps I would get it for her. She liked the suggestion and told him that she trusted him and the surgeon to do a good job. A few minutes later she was off to surgery.

A nurse showed me and Cameron where to wait and told us to stay there until we got a call from the operating room, letting us know that the surgery had begun. We got the call around noon. A few minutes later April joined us. At around 1:15 p.m. the surgeon called to tell us that the surgery went well and that Mia would not have to go to ICU. He would be sending her to recovery and from there back to a regular room on the neurology floor. He told us not to be alarmed when we saw the drainage tube he had inserted in her head; that it was routine and nothing to be concerned about.

While Mia was in recovery, we went down to the cafeteria to grab something to eat and then back up to the neurology floor to wait for transport to bring her to the room. When they brought her into the room she was awake and immediately reached for our hands to let us know that she was alright. Once the nurses got her settled in, she began talking and beckoned Cameron and April to stand by her bedside and just hold her hand for a few minutes. She was content and on the road to recovery.

Texts and phone calls were coming in. Several family members, including April, had been at an uncle's funeral and wanted to know how the surgery went. April updated them. Friends and co-workers were calling and texting so I sent out a couple of texts and the good news spread fast.

Later that afternoon the doctor came in and explained the surgery and what to expect post-operatively. His bottom line was that she had sailed through it with flying colors, and he didn't expect any complications. Before leaving, he asked Mia if she was glad to have her hard head back. She smiled and answered, "Yes." For her the term "hard head" took on a new meaning.

OUR GRATITUDE LESSON: Each day brings its own gifts. Sometimes they go unnoticed. Sometimes they are pleasant surprises. And sometimes they are disguised as pain, loss, and disappointment. Be grateful for them all.

YOUR GRATITUDE STORY: List five good things that today has brought to you.

July 14

An Early Discharge

 Mia

I am back at home with my head bandaged up, and I feel good. I had some new things to write in my gratitude journal, and the first one was that I left the hospital earlier than I expected. Even though the surgeon told me that putting my skull back on would be a piece of cake, I thought I would be there for a long time. He was right; the man knew what he was doing!

OUR GRATITUDE LESSON: Since coming home early was not something I expected, I had to add it to my journal twice – once for me and once for the good surgeon.

YOUR GRATITUDE STORY: What unexpected blessings have you experienced lately? What other people were involved? Did you thank them?

July 18

My Battle Scar

 MIA

The surgeon had told Mama when and how to take the bandage off my head. That way I wouldn't have to go back to the clinic to get it done. Today was the big day. I knew Mama could do, it but I was still nervous about it, and so was she. We both wanted to get it over with so after Mama gave me my morning meds I told her I was ready.

We went into the bathroom, and I sat down in my folding chair. Mama had everything laid out so I picked up my hand mirror and gave her a nod. As soon as she touched my head, I flinched, before she even took off one piece of tape. We both laughed. Then Mama told me to put the mirror down, or she would never get done. Once I put it down, it didn't take long, and it really didn't hurt at all. I remembered what the surgeon said: it would be a "piece of cake."

I grabbed the mirror again, turned my chair around, and took my time looking at the scar. I turned back and forth so I could see it from every angle. I couldn't believe it. "The man is good," I told Mama, looking back and forth from her to the mirror. "Look at the stitches; they are so neat. Perfect. You have to take some pictures so I can send them to my brothers and put them in my scrapbook. Now that I have my hard head back, I feel like I am complete again, like it's finally time for the real healing to begin."

OUR GRATITUDE LESSON: Every soldier has a battle scar and so do I. Mine is the scar that saved me, and I will honor it for the rest of my life.

YOUR GRATITUDE STORY: What battle scar(s) do you have? Write about it.

July 21

Friendship

 Mia

Today my friend Elizabeth picked me up and took me out to eat. We had a good time. She had taken me to therapy a few times, so she could see how I was getting better. It felt so good that she wanted to spend time with me.

I met Elizabeth in nursing school and we clicked. I think it was because of what I said to her the first day of class. I told her and a few other students that I was not there to hang out; I was there to graduate and move on with my life. Elizabeth said she felt the same way, and so we became friends.

One day when Elizabeth and her mom were visiting me in the hospital, her mother told Mama what I had said to the class on that first day, and we all laughed about it. Elizabeth visited me quite a bit. She always called first to see if I needed her to bring anything. A couple of times she stayed with me while Mama ran errands. She was a friend who didn't forget about me when I was down.

OUR GRATITUDE LESSON: The best time to make a friend is before you need one.

YOUR GRATITUDE STORY: List five qualities you love about your best friend. Thank her/him for sharing those qualities with you.

July 29

Television

 Myrtle

Watching TV all day is not a good recommendation for anyone, but neither is sitting around staring into space. Mia was doing a lot of staring and sleeping, and I had read enough about stroke patients to know that this was normal. So when she asked if it was possible for her to get a new TV, I was excited and grateful. The one she had was a gift from her grandmother over 30 years ago. It had served its purpose well, and it was definitely time for an upgrade.

As we talked about what kind we would get, I had a flashback to one evening in the hospital. It was Super Bowl Sunday, and one of the technicians thought he would cheer Mia up by bringing snacks to her room and watching the game with us. He walked into the room, flipped on the TV, and announced "We are going to have a Super Bowl party." Mia impolitely asked him to turn the TV off and leave. I could see the hurt and embarrassment on his face. He was just trying to be nice. What he didn't understand was that she couldn't stand the light or sound of the TV, therefore the Super Bowl game meant nothing to her. He gathered his things and quietly left.

To see some interest in TV return was another sign that her brain was healing. We went out, bought a new television, and Dwight installed it.

OUR GRATITUDE LESSON: Miracles don't always mean that mountains have to move. Sometimes they are slow and subtle, a sort of quiet healing.

YOUR GRATITUDE STORY: List five of your favorite TV shows. After each one write "thank you____________________for sharing your talent with me."

August 4

Love

I read Mia a fable from a magazine article I'd read, an article written by one of my favorite writers, Ron Fox. It was titled "You Make the Choice."

A woman comes out of her house and sees three old men with long white beards sitting in her yard. They look hungry, so she invites them in. But they inform her that they cannot come in until her husband returns home. When he returns, once again she invites them in. "We do not go into a house together," they reply. The woman asks why, and one of the men tells her, "One of us is Wealth, another is Success, and the third is Love. Go discuss with your husband which one of us you want to invite in."

The husband's first thought is to invite in Wealth. His wife disagrees and wants to invite in Success. Their daughter-in-law, who was observing the conversation, quickly interrupted and said, "Why not invite in Love? Then our home would be filled with Love."

They decide to follow the daughter-in-law's advice and invite in Love. As Love starts walking toward the house, the other two get up and follow him. The lady of the house was surprised and asked, "I only invited in Love. Why are all of you coming in?" The old men replied together: "If you had invited Wealth or Success, the other two would have stayed out. But since you invited Love, wherever he goes, we go with him. Wherever there is Love, there is also Wealth and Success."

I asked Mia which old man she would have chosen and I don't remember her answer but she understood the story and for now, that was all that mattered.

OUR GRATITUDE LESSON: Remove the barriers to love within yourself and you will find that love is the bridge to everything.

YOUR GRATITUDE STORY: List one problem you have and how it can be solved through love.

August 9

Cradle Cap and Baby Oil

 Mia

I went back to the neurologist today to get my stitches out. He had a good nurse and she promised she would be gentle and not make it hurt too much. I held Mama's hand and I think she ended up in as much pain as I did because I was squeezing her hand pretty hard. The three of us ended up laughing about it. The nurse told me I had "cradle cap" around my stitches, which was dry itchy dandruff like patches of skin that some newborn babies get. Mama remembered that after the first surgery a rehab nurse had used baby oil to get rid of it, so she stopped and picked up a bottle on the way home. We used it, and in a few days it was gone. Who said cradle cap only happened to babies?

OUR GRATITUDE LESSON: A $1.00 bottle of baby oil was a simple reminder that the more blessings I counted, the more I had to count.

YOUR GRATITUDE STORY: Look around the room and list five things that cost less than a dollar? Less than $5. Less than $10. How have those things been a blessing to you?

August 13

Digital Clocks

 MIA

I couldn't tell time. That bothered me. Since I had a new TV, I wanted to know what time my favorite shows came on. I couldn't understand the clocks with hands on them, so I asked Mama for a digital clock. She thought it was a good idea so she bought me one.

It didn't take long to figure out the "o'clock" because Mama gave me my medicine at 7 o'clock in the morning and at the same time at night. But I didn't know the difference between a.m. and p.m. and couldn't figure out how to match the time on the clock with the time a specific TV show came on. It was hard and Mama told me it would take a while to learn it again. She told me to think positively and to use 7:00 in the morning and 7:00 at night as a starting place. I had the new clock and was glad it was one more thing to add to my gratitude list.

OUR GRATITUDE LESSON: The longest journey begins with one single step. Be grateful for baby steps.

YOUR GRATITUDE STORY: Are you a good time manager? How would you manage your time if you couldn't tell time?

August 16

Index Cards

 Mia

Mama kept reading to me every night. She loved to use index cards to write on, and so she started writing positive sayings on brightly colored cards to help me with my reading and my thinking. She believed in positive thinking. I liked the cards and asked her to put some on the mirror, on the walls in my bathroom, and on my headboard. That way I could always see them. Sometimes when she was reading to me I would stop her right in the middle of the story and ask her to write down what she had just read. I started looking forward to her reading to me each night before bedtime.

OUR GRATITUDE LESSON: Your mind is like a garden; your thoughts are like seeds. In it you can grow flowers or you can grow weeds.

YOUR GRATITUDE STORY: Make a list of the positive thinkers you associate with. Make a list of the negative thinkers you associate with. With whom do you spend the most time?

August 25

A Lesson From an Old Friend

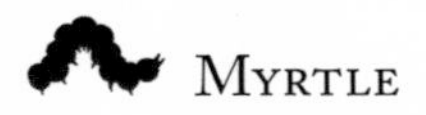

My friend Helen had kept in constant contact since Mia's stroke and had called to let me know that she was coming for a short visit. She had spent the last few weeks back and forth from Wisconsin to Atlanta to spend time with her new grandbaby. Helen was a seasoned traveler and since her retirement, I rarely heard from her. She was always busy and her busyness usually included travel and helping others.

"I'm tired of flying so I think I'll just drive to Chicago and catch the bus," she told me. I will come in on a Friday and spend the night and head back home Saturday evening. I just have to see Mia." That didn't make any sense to me, but it didn't have to; it was what she was going to do, and I knew whatever I said wouldn't matter.

It had been several years since Mia had seen Helen, so the visit was yet another reminder of how special she was. Once again, she commented, "Mama, I can't believe she is riding the bus all the way here to see me." I replied, "I can, it's just who she is."

Helen was her usual bubbly, inquisitive, loving self. We went to dinner at one of Mia's favorite restaurants. Before we ordered, she had given Mia a special gift that left Mia speechless for a few seconds, and then she came around with a "thank you." We enjoyed our meal and headed home to catch up and chat, staying up late. I was surprised that Mia joined us, but then Helen was as special to her as she is to me; later she told me that staying up wasn't hard.

The next morning we ended up going out of town to a funeral, so Helen got a chance to meet Warren, whose uncle had passed. Our plan was to go to the visitation and spend some time with family members. However, when we arrived at the church, we learned that the order of the service had changed, so we wouldn't have time to mingle. Nevertheless, it was Helen's nature to seize the moment so I introduced her to Warren by sharing with him how she had met his dad in the early 1970s, right after we married, and how much she liked and respected him, often referring to him as "smart and talented." Warren was always eager to hear good things about his dad so in just a few minutes, Helen had done what she does best: simply share her genuine loving self with everyone she meets. But our visit was brief. It was time for the funeral to start and we needed to get out of the way.

We left. During the drive back, Helen talked about how much Warren resembled his dad and how she wished she could have spent more time getting to know him. "Impossible with your schedule," I candidly reminded her. We chuckled.

We got back to Jackson, enjoyed lunch and went to the bus station. We got out of the car and took a few pictures and then got back in and talked, while waiting for the bus to arrive. While I was still hung up on her not staying long enough, Helen offered some words of wisdom: She reminded us that it was not the length of her stay that mattered most; it was the quality of the time we spent together. "We had two meals together. We got a chance to talk about old times when Mia last came to visit me. I got to meet Russell's oldest son, Warren. And we even got an unexpected treat – I got to drive through my pastor's hometown on the way to the funeral, something I had no idea I would do. And just think, I got to do it all with you Mia. Months ago we would not have done this, so at this point in my life, this visit is all that matters. Now I can go back home at peace with myself."

She had said enough. We noticed the Greyhound bus rounding the corner and got out of the car to get our last hugs. As Mia and I watched her strut toward the bus with her high heels clacking and her carry-on in tow, I thought about her parting words and how I needed to get them into my gratitude journal. Helen was indeed a wise and loving woman, and Mia and I agreed that we would not have traded that weekend for anything.

OUR GRATITUDE LESSON: Thank you God for using an old friend to teach me that sometimes it's what people don't know about each other that makes them such good friends.

YOUR GRATITUDE STORY: If you had to live on a remote island for a year and could only take one person with you, who would you take and why?

September 6

"Cut Loose"

 Mia

Today I had my last visit with the surgeon. He told me he was 'cutting me loose.' "You have been a model patient and there is no need for me to see you again. I believe you will do well." I thanked him and told him he was a good doctor and yes, I would be just fine. I asked him to write an order for more therapy for my right arm and hand, since they were still weak. He nodded, shook my left hand, and went to write the order. I haven't seen him since.

OUR GRATITUDE LESSON: Blessed are those who give without remembering and receive without forgetting.

YOUR GRATITUDE STORY: List five things you have given with no strings attached.

September 12

The Gift of Giving

MYRTLE

Mia heard that a young lady she went to high school with had had a stroke, and she wanted to reach out to her to see if she could give her some words of encouragement. She made reference to how nice people had been to her, so she wanted to do something good for someone else. I was more than happy to help her do that; besides, it would help me as well. This was confirmation that her gratitude journaling was paying off.

I called one of my classmates who was close to the young lady's family, and he was happy to connect us. A few days later we got a call from Mia's school mate saying how surprised she was to hear form us. "Ms. Russell," she said, "there are people who you thought cared about you and you never hear from them, so to have you and Mia contact me out of the blue; you just don't know how good that made me feel." She told me that she had heard about Mia's stroke and yes she'd had a stroke but it had not left her with any permanent paralysis. She shared some of the chronic conditions she had which included blindness, but I didn't detect one word of self-pity during the conversation. If anything, it was the total opposite. She expressed how grateful she was that the stroke had not left her paralyzed. She lived alone and wanted to continue to maintain her independence. Her strength was unbelievable for someone her age. Talk about putting things into proper perspective. Her spirit of gratitude and determination was palpable throughout the conversation; another indication that the three of us were supposed to connect.

I ended our conversation, handed the phone to Mia, and headed upstairs. They talked for a long time, sharing stories, laughing, and promising to keep in touch. After Mia hung up, she asked me to come back downstairs. "Mama, that girl can talk and I didn't know she was so funny. I didn't notice that when we were in school. But we didn't run in the same circle back then so I guess that's why. We put each other's numbers in our phones so we would definitely keep in touch. I need to talk to her because I don't think I could do what she is doing. I mean, how did she put my number in her phone and she is blind? And how will she know when I call her? She said she cooks for herself. How does she do all of that? I could not have made it through this stroke without you being here with me Mama. But she is blind and living by herself. I thought I would be helping her but she helped me." I reminded her that people show up in our lives for different reasons, and for now we could appreciate that we reached out to her and be grateful for the good that had already come about. "Yeap, I'm glad we did," she replied.

OUR GRATITUDE LESSON: Giving and receiving are two sides of the same coin.

YOUR GRATITUDE STORY: List three of the best gifts you've ever given to yourself?

September 21

Trust

MYRTLE

Our gratitude lists continued to grow. Today Mia would add climbing the stairs to her list. She had mentioned it several times before now but hadn't tried it, and to be honest it wasn't something I was enthusiastic about. I knew to get behind her when she was going up the stairs and in front of her when she was coming down, but all I could think about was - what if she fell?

"Mama, can I climb the stairs?" she asked after we finished dinner. She could tell by my facial expression that I wasn't thrilled about it. "You have to trust me," she said before I could answer. "How will I ever know if I don't just do it?" "You won't," I answered, "but it just makes me nervous." "I can do it Mama. I'll hold tight to the rails, just trust me." I reluctantly got behind her and motioned for her to go ahead. Very slowly, remembering what her physical therapist had taught her, she made the first step beginning with her strong left leg, and one step at a time she made it to the top. "I did it," she said, grinning. "See, I told you I could." I exhaled and gave her a big hug. "Now you have to go back down but let me get in front of you first." Descending stairs is scarier than climbing them, but she made it down just fine.

"See, I told you I could do it. You are just so scared," she said to me in a matter of fact tone. Then she was off to tell her brother about her accomplishment. It wasn't long before climbing stairs became a part of her daily routine.

OUR GRATITUDE LESSON: Nothing beats a failure but a try.

YOUR GRATITUDE STORY: List five things you are 100 percent certain you can do.

September 24

Letting Go

 MIA

When I came home from the hospital in March I needed a wheelchair, so the people at Mama's job were nice enough to let us borrow one. It's been eight months now and I walk with my cane, but sometimes I still use the wheelchair around the house, maybe just because it's here. On my brother's last visit, he asked me why I was still using it. I didn't have a good reason. He told me and Mama that it would become a crutch if we didn't get it out of the house. We agreed. It was good for me when I needed it but it was time to let it go. So one morning Mama got Uncle Dwight to load it into her car and she took it back to her job. I was grateful for my cane, so it made letting go of the chair a little easier.

OUR GRATITUDE LESSON: Accept what is, let go of what was, and have faith in what will be.

YOUR GRATITUDE STORY: Name one crutch you have a hard time letting go of. Why?

September 25

A Six Month Pass

MYRTLE

Mia had an appointment with the neurologist today and got good news - she didn't need to go back for six months. She hadn't had any more seizures, her lab work looked good, and she had made remarkable progress. "Yeeessss!" Mia shouted, pumping her fist in the air when she got the good news. When the doctor asked if we had any questions, Mia's only complaint was that she was still not sleeping well at night and needed a sleep aid. To my surprise the doctor suggested a natural sleep aid: melatonin. I wanted to stand up and shout "Yeeesss!" but I didn't. I was ecstatic when she suggested something natural. The last thing I wanted her to do was write a prescription for sleeping pills. Mia thanked her, and we were off to the health food store.

OUR GRATITUDE LESSON: Gratitude is wine for the soul. Drink up!

YOUR GRATITUDE STORY: Go back over your gratitude list and count the number of things you're grateful for since you started journaling. When you work on gratitude, gratitude works on you. Keep counting!

October 2

Staying Awake All Day

 MIA

Most people sleep at night and stay up during the day. Not me, and it was something Mama had to get used to. At first we thought maybe it was because I worked third shift before I had the stroke. But mama found out later through her reading that people who have strokes need lots of sleep in order for the brain to heal.

Today was another first for me; I got up at 10:30 in the morning and stayed up all day. "I think my brain is getting stronger," I said to Mama when she came home from work. It was a small change but I knew I was getting better.

OUR GRATITUDE LESSON: Man is the only animal that goes to bed when he is not sleepy and gets up when he is tired. Thank you stroke for teaching me to pay attention to what my brain and body are telling me.

YOUR GRATITUDE STORY: How many hours of sleep do you get each night? Is it too much or too little?

October 8

College Homecoming

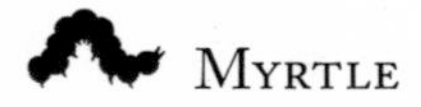

MYRTLE

This was homecoming weekend at Cameron and Mia's alma mater, the University of Tennessee at Chattanooga. Cameron insisted that we come and Mia was up for the ride. By 8:00 a.m. we were Chattanooga bound. We got there around noon and as is customary for Cameron, he had everything pretty much lined up. We started with lunch at one of our favorite restaurants and then headed on downtown for the homecoming festivities.

Cameron drove around several minutes looking for a parking space. All we saw was crowds of people, but no empty spaces. Mia and I gave each other that "we might as well leave" look, but didn't dare say anything. Cameron made a couple of phone calls and kept circling this one particular area. He finally spotted one of his friends who pointed us in the direction of a parking lot a few feet from their tailgate party. Cameron made the block once again and by the time we got to the parking lot, his friend was there to wave us in past a "DO NOT ENTER" sign. Finally, he parked, we got out, and like a child seeing the Christmas gift she'd been dreaming about all year long, Mia's face lit up with excitement.

She had not expected this, and neither had I. One of the first things I noticed was a huge grill that I learned was a 500-gallon propane tank that had been converted into a grill. The only place I had ever seen anything that size used for cooking was on TV. It was lined with briskets, hamburgers, polish sausages, and steaks. But the topper was that on one end of the grill was a large black cast iron pot where a young man stood battering filets of fish and dropping them into hot sizzling oil. "We know you like fish Ms. Russell, so we got you some cooking," Cam's friend Robert said to me with a welcoming smile. Watching another friend master the grill was like watching a barbeque cook-off on TV. In about 10 minutes the fish was ready, and all I needed was a Coke and a seat. Cameron's friend made sure I had both. Talk about good eats! It was the best I'd eaten at a cookout.

Mia, on the other hand, wasn't interested in food. She couldn't believe her eyes when she saw roommates she hadn't seen in 15 years. A few of them didn't know about her stroke, and one started to cry when she hugged Mia, but Mia wasn't having it. She told her not to feel sorry for her, that she was getting better and that was all that mattered. Her roommate quickly wiped away the tears and they sat down and began reminiscing.

The guys kept coming over to offer Mia food but she was too busy taking it all in. The last surprise was Warren and his wife. They had been tailgating several blocks away, but Cameron let them know that we were there. Mia had no idea they were in town. When she saw them, her face lit up again.

It was a beautiful weekend and our four-hour drive home seemed shorter than usual, mostly because Mia talked about the tailgate party all the way home. Since the stroke, if we were on a long trip, she was asleep 30 minutes after we got on the interstate, but not this time. And every single day for the next two weeks she mentioned something about the trip. She had taken pictures and once we got home and settled, she posted a couple to her Facebook page. She also printed one and asked me to add it to her scrapbook. She praised Cameron for his persistence in getting her to the tailgate party, despite parking obstacles. Several times she mentioned how Warren's being there was icing on the cake. She talked about the friends who took time to sit down and talk to her and ask her how she was really doing. And even though she didn't eat anything, she said she couldn't get the size of the grill and the picture of all the food out of her head.

Talk about therapeutic! Nothing clinical could have trumped this homecoming weekend experience and Cameron knew it when he insisted that we make the trip.

OUR GRATITUDE LESSON: Nothing heals like the human touch.

YOUR GRATITUDE STORY: When's the last time you attended any kind of "homecoming?" List five things you enjoyed.

October 10

Sharing Good Memories

 Mia

I couldn't wait to tell my therapist about my trip to Chattanooga. I showed the staff pictures and the video that Robert had sent me. When Mama came to pick me up, my therapist told her, "Mia had her best session ever today so I guess she needs to go to Chattanooga more often." We laughed.

"I showed them something today mama," I told Mama when we got in the car. "I see," she said. "I guess we do need more "Chattanooga weekends." We had another good laugh.

OUR GRATITUDE LESSON: Add and multiply your joy, then share it with others.

YOUR GRATITUDE STORY: What is the last piece of good news you shared? Who did you share it with? What makes you feel better, sharing good news or bad news?

October 21

Anger

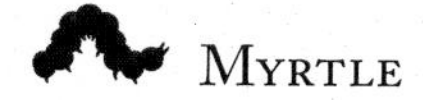

MYRTLE

As I've mentioned before, this journey has not been without some weary days. Sadness has stolen a few days, and occasionally, loneliness has shown up, uninvited. On most days when these unwelcomed guests visited, I journaled or talked to a friend. Mia rarely noticed any change in my attitude or behavior. But anger got the best of me today, and I made Mia the target. In hindsight, the incident that perpetuated my anger was trivial. My giving her a piece of my mind didn't lead to peace. It was just the opposite. We didn't talk for almost 24 hours after I exploded, and that was not a good feeling.

By the end of the second day I realized that my rage was about blaming her for becoming ill, as if she had chosen to have the stroke. I knew I had to do something, and I knew exactly what it was. I had to say I was sorry and mean it. Apologies are one thing; it's what you do after the apology that really matters. I needed to never again have to say "I'm sorry" for hurting her feelings (or anyone else's) with harsh words, or as my mother would often say, "Don't let that red rag in your mouth get you into trouble."

So I went to her room, sat down on her bed, and told her I was sorry. I explained to her that parents can be wrong and I was wrong for the way I spoke to her. She accepted my apology and said she was also sorry for what she had done. She told me that she understood why I was upset with her but the way I talked to her made her feel stupid and dumb. We talked for a while longer and agreed that we felt better.

I went upstairs and journaled about my foolishness. As I wrote, I reminded myself that moving forward, my actions would be the best demonstration of just how sorry was. I realized that when you're angry, yes you might feel better after you've mouthed off, had your say, and put that person in her/his place, but if you have a heart, you'll regret it. Regret is a thief that can rob you of your joy.

OUR GRATITUDE LESSON: When you're angry, take a lesson from the astronauts: Always count down before blasting off!

YOUR GRATITUDE STORY: When has anger caused you to hurt someone? Did you ask for forgiveness?

November 9

A Time to Remain Silent

 MYRTLE

Today marks ten months since the stroke. Mia is making remarkable progress, however, life's questions keep hounding me. I wonder what Mia's future would look like. Will she be able to live alone and take care of herself again? Will she be totally independent again? Will her social security disability check be enough to take care of her? If not, who would pick up the slack when I'm gone? Had Cameron thought about her future? Could he/would he take care of her? She had often talked about moving back to Chattanooga so subconsciously, was this what was unfolding? What does my future hold? When will I leave my job since I already know that my retirement income would not add up to what I wanted it to be? What about the golden years I had dreamed of as a writer?

I knew I had to put these questions in my journal and leave them there for now. Time and prayer would bring the answers. I also knew I needed to be paying attention so I could recognize the answers when they showed up. The mind could be tricky, like a lethal weapon when allowed to run amok with negative thoughts. I had to stay focused on the positive, regardless of the questions or the circumstances. If I was being judged by the questions that popped up in my head this morning, I might have been deemed brilliant, but judge me by my answers and I was merely a lost soul seeking direction.

It was ironic that Mia also had questions, many of which were similar to mine. Here are the questions she asked: "Do you still have my name on your insurance policies? What will happen to me when you die? You know you are getting older so we have to talk about these things. If my hand and arm and brain don't get better, I can live with that, but I may not be able to live alone, so where would I go, who will help take care of me? Do you think I should talk to my brothers? Do you think I will ever meet a man who loves me the way I am now? What do you think Mama?"

Mercy. I told her they were tough questions, questions I had thought about as well, but I didn't have all the answers. "I have written them in my journal and I am claiming guidance," I said, and I suggested she do the same thing. "I know you have a hard time writing so if you want help, you know I will help when you are ready." I also told her it was okay to share her questions with Cameron, and if he saw the need to talk to Warren, then he would make that happen. She was okay with that. The last thing I told her was, "we'll keep praying for guidance." Then I went upstairs, got in bed, and cried. I asked joy to meet me in the morning. It was the best I could do.

OUR GRATITUDE LESSON: You can't do much with faith alone, but without it, you can do nothing.

YOUR GRATITUDE STORY: What do you do when you are hounded by questions that seemingly have no answers?

November 9

A Time to Speak

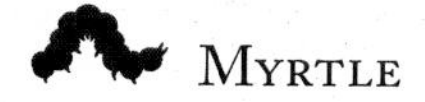

MYRTLE

Mia shared her questions with Cameron today, but she didn't get the answers she expected. His answer was along these lines: "Don't worry about those things right now. Instead put all of your energy into getting better, and we'll cross those bridges when we get to them." Her reply: "Yeah...you're right."

Later, Cameron and I talked about her questions, and he reminded me of a few basic spiritual principles that led to his answering the way he did. He mentioned the law of averages, which says that I would have had a stroke before Mia, but I hadn't, so who's to say who will die first? He pointed out the law of attraction, which says what we think about we bring about, be it good or bad, so he didn't think it was a good idea to waste energy worrying about what would happen to Mia when I die. For now, we were all alive, which meant we had something to work with. He reminded me of the law of action that states one must engage in actions that support his or her dreams. Therefore, collectively the best thing we could do was to continue to encourage Mia, remain positive, do the work that supports her dreams, and let time take care of the rest. He said he knew that this was a tall order, and yes there needed to be some more things in place but for now, we had to keep moving. We had to keep seeking God's guidance and keep believing that the answers would come.

OUR GRATITUDE LESSON: "You'll be happy to know that the universal law that created miracles hasn't been repealed." -Wayne Dyer

YOUR GRATITUDE STORY: List five little miracles that have occurred in your life over the last five years.

November 8

A Lap Desk

 MYRTLE

Mia asked me if I would buy her a lap desk similar to the one I use to journal in bed. This was another prayer answered so I put it at the top of our "to do" list for today.

We made an afternoon run to the bookstore, and Mia was surprised at the number of lap desks to choose from. She looked at several and decided on one with the inscription: "Pray More, Worry Less." I love bookstores and could have easily stayed there for hours but Mia was anxious to get home and use her new desk. Driving home, I couldn't help but wonder where she might have been had she taken journaling seriously years ago. Of course I'll never know, but I believed that it would play a major role in her healing. I could not be more excited that she was giving it a try.

OUR GRATITUDE LESSON: "Let me embrace thee, sour adversity, for wise men say it is the wisest course." -William Shakespeare

YOUR GRATITUDE STORY: Think of one negative that you can turn into a positive by trying something different.

November 11

Kindergarten Books

 Mia

I had started working in word search books, and I liked how they made me work harder. Mama and the therapists said my brain needed the challenge. "Don't you think it's time for me to work on something else to help me with reading?" I asked Mama? She reminded me that we still had the activity books she bought when I was in the hospital. She found five Pre-K and Kindergarten books. I told her I wanted to work on one page from each book every day and I got started.

I worked in the books during the day and each night after dinner mama would go over my work. Mostly what I did was write and say my ABCs and my numbers. It made me think about when I was in grade school and she would check my homework. I was just as happy to get the answers right as I was back then. I knew I was doing a good job, so I asked Mama how long she thought it would take me to read again. "I don't know, but what I do know is that if you keep working at it, it will happen. You will read again," she told me every time I asked. I couldn't remember what came after kindergarten so Mama had to explain it to me. She told me it wouldn't be long before I would be doing first grade work. I was proud of myself.

It was funny that before the stroke, I had never thought about kindergarten books. Most people don't. But here I was like a child, excited about them.

OUR GRATITUDE LESSON: Reading is fundamental!

YOUR GRATITUDE STORY: What is one thing you could do for a person who can't read?

November 16

A Good Gynecologic Exam

 MIA

Today I had to go and get the exam that every woman hates - a pap smear I hated it even more this time because of the stroke. I told Mama I was afraid. I couldn't figure out how I was going to get up on the table. How would I get my feet in those things (stirrups Mama called them) at the end of the table and open my legs? I couldn't make my right leg and foot do all of that because it seemed like they had a mind of their own. "I just won't be able to do it," I said to Mama when we got to the clinic. "Yes, you can. I will be there with you and so will the doctor and a nurse. The three of us can help so you'll be fine," she said to me, trying to make me feel better. It didn't work.

When my doctor walked into the room he had his head down looking at my chart. I had been seeing him for 20 years. He had a confused look on his face when he looked up at me and then asked, "When did this happen?" Right away, without even thinking about it, I answered "January 9." I looked at Mama and she was grinning. He looked me in the eye and said "I'm so sorry," and reached out to hold my left hand. That was one reason Mama and I liked him; he showed that he cared. As Mama would often say, "He was not the type of doctor who treated you as if you were just another number." Then he asked me: "Do they know what caused it?' I told him that we didn't know. He asked a few more questions and handed me that ugly blue paper gown and told me to put it on. Before he left the room, he asked if I needed help getting on the exam table. "My Mama will help me," I told him.

He closed the door. I started taking my clothes off and asked Mama to help me with my bra. Before she did she asked: "Do you know what you just did?" You just gave the doctor the exact date you had the stroke? Can you believe that?" "I couldn't believe it either, Mama," I said. "It just came out, just like that. I didn't even think about it. You know before I could never answer. I wonder why I knew the answer this time." We didn't know it, but it couldn't have happened at a better time because it made what would happen next a little bit easier.

Mama helped me with the gown and getting up on the table. When the doctor and nurse came back in, he helped me get in the right position. He told me to relax my knees. That wasn't easy, but I did it after a few tries. He did what he was good at and I got through the exam. He had a way of helping you relax because he talked to you while he was examining you. I liked that. Mama said she liked him because he had a gentle, warm spirit.

After he finished, Mama helped me get dressed. "So, that wasn't as bad as I thought it would be," I told her as we left the clinic. "I told you could do it," she reminded me, still grinning about how I remembered the date I had the stroke. We left there with some new things to put in our gratitude journals. It was the best Pap smear I ever had, if there is such a thing.

OUR GRATITUDE LESSON: Pleasant surprises can occur in unlikely places, at unlikely times, sometimes sparked by unlikely questions. Welcome them!

YOUR GRATITUDE STORY: Who is your favorite doctor? The next time you visit, let them know why they are your favorite. If you want to multiply your blessings, do something nice for the staff.

November 23

A Meaningful Thanksgiving

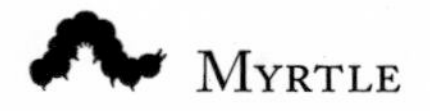

Myrtle

Thanksgiving this year was different. It was a Thanksgiving of "firsts." For Mia it was the first Thanksgiving since she had the stroke. It was her first time to talk about how good things were before she had the stroke and how little she had appreciated them. It was the first time the two of us had ever discussed the true meaning of being thankful. For the first time she shared with me that even though she wasn't able to do some of the things we had traditionally done before the stroke, she still had a lot to be thankful for.

This was the first time in six years that we wouldn't be making our trip to New York to visit family, so we talked about what we would miss most about the trip. At the top of Mia's list was pizza. For her, nobody made pizza like New Yorkers. It was the first thing she ate when she got there and the last thing she ate before leaving.

For me Thanksgiving in New York was about spending the day at Marvin and Gloria's home. There was always a steady flow of family and friends. It was a time of storytelling, laughter, and reminiscing. And then there was the traditional Thanksgiving dinner. Everyone that walked through their door had their mouths watering for Gloria's "baked macaroni" as she called it. It was definitely my favorite dish. And the table was not complete without Marvin's turkey. The man took as much pride in carving his signature turkey as he did in cooking it. Conversations ceased as he removed the apple from the turkey's cavity, rubbed his fork and knife together a few times, and meticulously went to work on that bird as if he was getting paid to do it. He took his time, placing the slices of meat on the platter, careful to separate the white meat from the dark. By the time he finished, we were all standing in line like children waiting to be served. It was a festive evening that carried over into the early morning hours.

Another highlight of the trip was the day after Thanksgiving and the excitement of riding the subway to Manhattan to shop and enjoy ethnic foods that could only be dished up on the streets of New York City, which were always bustling with an energy I call eclectic. For months we would save our money to shop. Like the food, the shopping was unmatched. There was something on the streets for every person's pocketbook. We bought things at a third of the price we would have paid for them at home. We had my brothers, Timmy and Kevin, who lived there to thank for that. They knew the hot spots. We laughed about how we always left the city loaded down with bags, which wasn't a good thing when you're trying to catch a subway train. They helped us manage and we always made it back to Yonkers just before dark, but not before a stop at a pizza joint.

We always enjoyed the drive from Tennessee to New York, which meant 16 hours of family bonding. Our contribution to the Thanksgiving dinner was honey baked hams, so our pit stops included checking our cooler to be sure that the glaze on the hams wasn't melting. We couldn't deliver ruined hams to friends, although I think they would have eaten them anyway.

Getting closer to New York meant the anticipated excitement of crossing the George Washington Bridge. The first year we made the drive, Cameron learned how important it was to make the last bathroom pit stop before leaving New Jersey. Even though the bridge is just short of a mile long and has an upper and lower deck consisting of 14 lanes on each deck, because of the heavy volume of cars inching across the bridge at a snail's pace at that time of year, having a full bladder could be torturous, leaving you with only a couple of options: pee in your clothes or find something in the car to pee in. Cameron chose the latter. We still laugh about it. It was one of those times when we were all grateful for a paper cup and a window to throw it out of.

Yes, this Thanksgiving would be different. Mia's stroke forced us to examine the word "Thanksgiving" for what we thought it really should be, a way of living not one day or one weekend out of the year, but every day. It should be about recognizing that each day comes bearing gifts; gifts that often go unnoticed and unappreciated. Sometimes the gifts are little unexpected surprises and sometimes they are disguised as pain, loss, and disappointment. Since we would not be traveling to New York this year, we decided that an attitude of gratitude would be the best way to spend this Thanksgiving weekend.

We didn't have the traditional Thanksgiving meal but everyone enjoyed what we had. Mia helped with the preparation. With her left hand and a little assistance from me, she made her signature brownies. Grateful. Even though she could not peel and cut up the potatoes, she showed me how to make the best candied yams I ever made. It was another dish she had mastered. Grateful! We had a steady flow of family throughout the day, it was the first time we had spent Thanksgiving with them in six years. Grateful! Mia's helping out in the kitchen was a boost to her confidence, and she felt that the stroke was only a temporary setback. For the first time she was discovering the new Mia and she talked about how good it felt. Grateful!

OUR GRATITUDE LESSON: Don't look at what you have lost; instead appreciate what you have left.

YOUR GRATITUDE STORY: List five things you can do to make every day a thanksgiving day.

November 26

Wonder

 MIA

I wanted to see the movie Wonder. "I think it will be good," I told Mama one night after I saw it advertised on TV. Mama thought it looked good too and said we would go on Saturday. We both liked it. I laughed. I cried. I learned something. Mama doesn't go to the movies much, but she said Wonder was the type of movie she could watch again.

After the movie we went to eat. While we were waiting for our food, I told Mama why I wanted to see the movie and how thankful I was that we watched it together. I told her that I could understand Auggie, the ten-year-old boy who was born with a disease called Treacher Collins syndrome, which made his face look different from that of other people his age. The way kids stared at Auggie on his first day of school reminded me of the way people stared at me when I had to wear my helmet. Even after I had stopped wearing the helmet, they still look at me strangely because I walk with a cane. I also drag my right foot, and my right arm and hand kind of dangle and swing back and forth when I walk. They appear to feel sorry for me but don't know what to say. I hate that, and sometimes I just want to shout "boo" to see what they would do. Yes, I could see why Auggie wanted to keep his face covered in public because to be stared at was not a good feeling.

Auggie didn't have a lot of friends. I understood that too. Even though several friends showed up when I had the stroke, most of them were now moving on with their lives. I asked Mama why. Here is how she explained it. "For the most part, people care and it's just their nature to show up in a time of crisis for various reasons. Some show up to see what you look like. Others want to see how bad things are so that they can go back and tell their friends and family what they saw, or thought they saw." We laughed. Mama can say things in a funny way and you can't help but laugh, even if it is something that is supposed to be sad or serious. She went on to say that co-workers come to let you know that they miss you and hope you can come back to work soon. Some friends show up because it's the "Christian" thing to do. Family members show up because it's what families do, and they're usually glad to do whatever they can to help. But what all of these people have in common is that after a short while, they get back to their lives; and their everyday routine. Not because they no longer care, but because for the most part they have to. They have families and jobs and obligations that don't stop because you are sick. You have to keep in mind that you are the one who cannot keep up with them and that is a something you have to accept. But there are a handful of people who will be there for you regardless. They will always show up at the right time, do the right thing, and expect nothing in return.

She gave me some names to help me understand what she meant. Then she asked me a question: "How did it make you feel when all the people came to see you in the hospital?" "It felt good. I was shocked. I didn't know that many people cared about me," I told her. "Then hold on to that feeling and believe that the right people will keep showing up when you need them just as they did back then and just as they did for Auggie, and you will be just fine.

I asked Mama what was her favorite part of the movie. She waited for a couple of seconds. "I could relate to his mother and the sacrifices she made for her son. She was a writer and you know I like to write, right?" she asked me. I nodded. "Well, his mother put her writing on hold because of Auggie's condition and so did I. You know I had paid to go to a writing conference in North Carolina in February of 2017. It was a birthday present to me, but I cancelled it after you had the stroke. Auggie's mother got back to her writing after he adjusted in school and I will get back to mine as you continue to progress. And besides, now I have a new story, our story." Mama gave me what she would call a "reassuring" smile and thanked me for suggesting the movie. She said it was one of the best she had ever seen. We kept laughing and talking about our favorite scenes while we ate our dinner.

The next day Mama told me that she woke up thinking about the movie and how it gave her a few more things to add to her gratitude list. She said it was a "wonder" that she came home on January 9th and found me on the floor, still conscious after lying in the floor for hours. It was a "wonder" that she noticed the change in my status four days after the stroke and alerted the nurse to contact the neurologist. It was a "wonder" that I survived two surgeries. It was a "wonder" that I wanted to see the movie. It was a "wonder" that I could explain what I liked about the movie. And it was a "wonder" that I had not given up on life.

OUR GRATITUDE LESSON: A good movie should do two things: make you forget you're sitting in the theater; and cause you to leave feeling better than you did when you came. Wonderful!

YOUR GRATITUDE STORY: List three of your favorite movies and why they were worth two hours of your time?

December 6

Mama, I Remember Your Name

 MIA

Mama was upstairs crocheting when I yelled out "Myrtle Delores Russell." "Yes?" she answered. I said it again, as loud as I could. I heard her running down the steps. When she got to my door, I was sitting up in my bed giggling. "You didn't know I remembered your name did you Myrtle Delores Russell? Busted your bubble didn't I Myrtle Delores Russell?" Mama gave me a big hug. "I don't know what made my brain do that," I said, "but I'm glad it did." It was another little miracle.

OUR GRATITUDE LESSON: Happiness is never denied the person who calls it forth with praise and thanksgiving.

YOUR GRATITUDE STORY: If you had to choose between following your brain and following your heart, which would you choose? Why?

December 9

Reading, Writing, and Arithmetic

 Mia

I'm doing better with reading, writing, and arithmetic. When I write in my journal and on index cards, I can now write inside the lines. Before, all my letters went downhill. Today I started new first grade spelling and math workbooks. I also read half of a quote from one of my Word Find books. I think music therapy has a lot to do with it. Also Mama reminded me that the brain heals by doing something over and over again, so the more time I spend on my workbooks, the better I will get. It feels good to know I went from not knowing my ABCs to first grade workbooks in eleven months.

OUR GRATITUDE LESSON: First I learned to read. Then I read to learn. Now I'm learning to read again. Thank God for second chances.

YOUR GRATITUDE STORY: What was your favorite subject in school? Would it be your favorite if you couldn't read?

December 10

"Thank You" Christmas Cards

 Mia

Mama and I had talked about making Christmas cards to send to family and friends to say "thank you," so today we went to see what we could find. I picked the design and since Mama is much better with words, she wrote the message. It was a short poem. Mama likes to write poetry. With a little help from a store associate, we finished the card and shopped while she printed them.

When we got home, Mama started working on the mailing list. She had kept every card I received since I had the stroke, so it was easy to make a mailing list. She wrote the addresses on the cards and put them in the envelopes. I put the stamps and return address labels on the envelopes.

Working with the cards reminded me of when I was little girl and how much I liked adding machines. I would ask for one every Christmas and I also got my own notepads and ink pens. I think I got one about four years in a row. Whenever Mama went shopping, I would ask for the receipts and sit at the kitchen table and use my adding machine to check to see if the totals on the receipts were right. I liked adding anything with numbers. It didn't take long for me to finish off the roll of paper that came with the adding machine. Then I had to ask Mama to buy more paper. For years, no matter what I got at Christmas, I always wanted an adding machine. Helping Mama with the Christmas cards just took me back to that childhood feeling of helping her. It felt like I put my heart into it, just as Mama had done.

I recognized some names on the cards but there were some people I had never met or didn't remember. Mama took the time to tell me a little about each person that I didn't recognize. It took us a few days. We ended up with 70 cards but it wasn't enough, so we ordered some more. Each card was a good reminder of how much we had to be thankful for this holiday season.

OUR GRATITUDE LESSON: The poem Mama chose for our Christmas card:

> *"We have lots of people to be thankful for*
> *One of them is you.*
> *You make our journey more meaningful*
> *By the loving things you do.*
> *Best of Holidays*
> *Mia and Myrtle*

YOUR GRATITUDE STORY: What was your favorite Christmas toy when you were a child? Why was it your favorite?

December 15

My Brain and My Heart: A Good Mix

 MIA

I had been following my brother and one of his boxing clients on Twitter and Facebook and downloading his pictures to my phone. I knew how much Cameron loved working with his new young client. His client was 11 years old when Cameron met him and it was at that time that he told Cameron he wanted to be a professional boxer. He is 25 years old now and he knew that Cameron was good at what he did because he had worked with some of the best athletes in the country. So he became one of Cameron's trainees. I wanted to do something special for Cameron and the pictures would be a good reminder for him to be grateful for what he wanted to accomplish with this up and coming boxer. Mama said what I was doing was making a vision board for him. At that time, his client had not lost a fight.

So I downloaded pictures of some his client's fights, pictures that Cameron was in, and emailed them to the store to be printed. Then I had to go to the store to be sure they had printed the right sizes. April and I took care of that. I also had to get the right frame, so today Mama took me shopping for the perfect frame.

It didn't take long to find a frame I liked. I asked Mama what she thought about it. She liked it, so I took a picture of it on my phone and went to pay for it. "This is going to be the perfect gift. I know Cameron will like it," I said to Mama while we were standing in the checkout line. I knew it would fit in with the other sports memorabilia (Mama's word) he had on his walls. His client Peyton Manning and his autographed pictures and Super Bowl shadow boxes took up quite a bit of space. But one of the first pictures you saw when you walked into his living room was of 'The Greatest,' Muhammad Ali. From childhood, Cameron loved Ali and talked about how much he respected him. I figured these new pictures could go next to Ali's. One picture was of his client and Cameron holding championship belts from a 2017 HBO fight. I also included a picture of Cameron with a retired boxer, Roy Jones who was what Mama called a commentator at his last championship fight in California. Yep, I knew he would like his gift. Christmas couldn't come soon enough.

"When I go to pick up these pictures, it's going to take a while because they have to be perfect," I said to Mama after we got home and I went through the pictures I had chosen. "They are all the same size, but not the same shape - you know what I mean?" I asked Mama. She nodded.

April and I went to pick up the pictures, and when we got there the pictures were not the way I wanted them to be. I said to the clerk, "no problem." I pulled out my phone and showed her a picture of the frame; the picture I took on the day that Mama took me to buy it. "I need the pictures to fit this frame," I told her. We waited for her to reprint them. I left the store with exactly what I wanted.

Later that night when I worked on my gratitude list, I had to ask Mama how to spell some new words like 'Christmas' and a new word she had taught me: 'collage'." She told me she was so proud of me for making the perfect gift without her help. She said it was proof that my brain was slowly getting better. By the end of the week, the gift was ready and I was ready for Christmas.

OUR GRATITUDE LESSON: What you give from the heart cannot return to you empty. It lands you in a good place, regardless of the circumstances.

YOUR GRATITUDE STORY: List three of the most meaningful gifts you've received as an adult. Why were they so meaningful? List three of the most meaningful gifts you've ever given. How did giving them make you feel?

December 25

Priceless Christmas Gifts

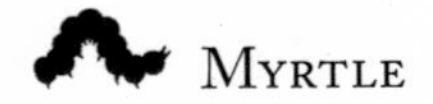 Myrtle

Christmas is my favorite holiday. This year, like Thanksgiving, things would be different. Our friends from New York had planned to spend Christmas with us since they hadn't seen Mia since she had the stroke, but they ended up having to cancel. We were looking forward to seeing them but we understood. It ended up being just the three of us and we were definitely going to make it a good Christmas, filled with priceless gifts.

Like anxious children, we got up early. Mia, who never liked getting up early was surprisingly awake and ready to keep the Christmas tradition going. For the last 11 months, sleeping in had become the norm for her, so I was happy to see her get up early with a smile on her face. Cameron had to have his favorite caffeine fix so we had to wait for him to return from Starbucks to open gifts. When he walked through the door, coffee in hand, Mia was ready. We both had the gift of patience.

Tradition was that I opened my gifts first, Mia next, and Cameron last. We had long stopped buying gifts just for the sake of giving, so it was always exciting to see where our hearts and heads were each Christmas. Books and practical things always pleased me. Mia had given me her gift a few days before Christmas. On the day that we were getting the frame for Cameron's pictures, we passed a table of ceramic snowmen on our way to the checkout counter. She knew I liked snowmen, so when I stopped and picked one up to look at it, she commented that it was cute and asked me if I was going to get it. I told her I was and placed it in the shopping cart. "It's cute," she said. "Yep," I replied, "I'm buying it for myself for Christmas." When we got to the checkout counter she told the cashier that she was paying for the snowman and the frame, and she turned to me to ask me to help her count her money. My pleasure. I was grateful that she had money to count and a heart to give. After the clerk bagged our items, I smiled and humbly said, "Thank you."

The snowman sat in the center of the table among the others I'd collected over the years. She pointed it out to Cameron and told him how proud she was to remember that I liked snowmen and to be able to pay for it with her own money. That got a wink and a smile from her big brother. Another gift!

Mia was all smiles as she opened her gifts and she liked them all, especially the gift cards. However it was obvious that her favorite was WHATCHAMACALLIT candy bars from Cameron. Pronouncing words was an ongoing struggle, and sometimes she gave up and just said, "Whatchamacallit." We teased her about it and sometimes when she asked me a question, I would reply, "you know, uh, whatchamacallit," She always laughed. It also made her more mindful the next time she was tempted to say it. Only her brother would go to the trouble of finding the candy bars that I didn't even know still existed. Neither did Mia. When she pulled the candy bar out of the bottom of her bag, her mouth flew open and she just stared at it. "What is it?" Cameron asked. She looked back and forth from him to the candy bar a couple of times before blurting out: "Whatchamacallit." We all laughed. What a gift!

Now on to the finale; it was Cameron's turn to open his gifts, and Mia made sure that he opened hers last. It wasn't in a box or bag, nor was it neatly wrapped. With one hand she simply covered it with wrapping paper and put tape on it to hold it together as best she could. For her it was the content that mattered.

Ripping off the first piece of paper, Cameron's eyes grew big. His smile said he knew he was unwrapping something special. The more paper he ripped off, the glassier his eyes became. By the time he removed all the paper, tears were trickling down his face. For what seemed like a very long time, he sat there staring at the pictures. Mia and I looked at each other and grinned. Then he stood up, walked over to Mia, hugged her tightly, and tears trickled down his cheeks. Mia looked over his shoulder at me and our grins disappeared, replaced with tears of joy. Another priceless gift!

When he finally let go of Mia, he looked at me and said, "Mother, I appreciate your gifts, but I'm sorry, this one trumps everything." I told him I knew it would, that my gifts paled in comparison, and my feelings weren't hurt a bit. Wiping our faces, we chuckled. He then turned to Mia and asked, "How did you know how to do this? Did Mama help you?" "Nope," we both answered in unison. "I knew she was doing it but she told me right up front that she didn't want my help except to get a frame, so I left it to her." I added. He sat there holding the frame in disbelief. "Where did you find this picture of me and Roy Jones," he asked? "I didn't send it to you." "From your Twitter page," Mia told him. "But I didn't even know you were following me that closely. Man. You have shocked me. For someone who's had a stroke like yours to be able to think of this is unreal, out of the ordinary."

No, there was absolutely nothing ordinary about Mia's recovery. Her first Christmas was nothing short of a culmination of little miracles, not only for her but for the family. Yes, there had been glitches in our initial plans, and yes, she had some limitations, but none of that could steal her Christmas joy. A new Mia was blossoming, and today was yet another reminder that each day comes with its own gifts, its own little miracles.

OUR GRATITUDE LESSON: Difficulty plants the seeds for miracles, love causes them to grow.

YOUR GRATITUDE STORY: Do you have a Christmas tradition? Journal about it.

January 9, 2018

A Year of Miracles

Mia & Myrtle

Miracles occur where the invisible possibilities of life unfold as realities.
– Bernie Siegal, M.D

Today marks one year since the stroke, and this book is our celebration of all the good we've experienced. I knew I had to share our gratitude story, but what I didn't know back then was the number of little miracles that would unfold along the way. Even though not everyone defines miracles the same way, they are found in all major world religions and spiritual practices. Christmas and Easter are stories of miracles. Conception and childbirth are miracles. The seasons, sunrise, sunset, the galaxy, oceans, mountains, and rainbows; they are all miracles. One has to look no further than nature to see miracles at their best, occurring every single day, some big and some small. In addition to the miracles already chronicled in this book, here are a few more things the journey taught and brought us:

- Love inspires miracles; everything derived from love is a miracle.
- Prayer is the medium to manifest miracles; we prayed and our prayers were answered.
- Faith is belief in miracles. We never stopped believing and seeing miracles unfold.
- Expectancy is the atmosphere for miracles; we expected the best.
- Work is the companion of miracles; God worked through all the people who showed up for us in so many ways.

- Courage is the foundation for miracles; we knew we had to act boldly.
- Dreams are the images of miracles; they were our previews of coming attractions.
- Intention is the reason for miracles; our intentions became our reality.
- Intuition is the internal indicator that miracles are about to happen; we learned to listen.
- Joy is a miracle worker's contentment; it was a gauge that kept us motivated.
- Gratitude is the highest form of appreciation for miracles; we are now living by it.

The Guest House - Rumi

This being human is a guest house.
Every morning a new arrival.

A joy, a depression, meanness,
some momentary awareness comes
as an unexpected visitor.

Welcome and entertain them all!
Even if they're a crowd of sorrows,
who violently sweep your house
empty of its furniture,
still, treat each guest honorably.
He may be clearing you out
for some new delight.

The dark thought, the shame, the malice,
meet them at the door laughing,
and invite them in.

Be grateful for whoever comes,
because each has been sent
as a guide from beyond.

Thank you Mia for bringing me new meaning to this poem!

MIA'S CLOSING:

Just like I believed a year ago that Mama would come home and save me, now I believe more good days are ahead. Little miracles keep happening, here are just a few more:

- When I left the hospital on March 2, 2017, I didn't know my ABCs. Now I'm working in fourth and fifth grade books.
- I go to the gym three days a week. Most days I walk a mile.
- My speech is getting better, and I don't get as frustrated when the words don't come out right. As Mama always reminds me, people know what I mean.
- I can count money and pay for what I buy, all by myself.
- Not only are my prayers being answered, but my prayers for others as well. Just ask my Uncle Jerome. We have blessed each other with little miracles.
- I have set two goals for myself: to drive again, and to go back to college. I will do them both or die trying.
- And I have to add this: Mama and Cousin Sandra tried to plan a surprise birthday celebration for me. It was going to be part of this book signing. The surprise party part of the plan didn't work. Three days after they started planning, I knew something wasn't right so I asked Mama two questions: If the book signing includes me, why didn't you take me with you and Cousin Sandra to look at the place where you were planning to have it? And the second question was when was I going to read the book if she expected me to choose the title? Those two questions forced her to tell me the truth. We laughed about it and things went a lot more smoothly after that.

For years Mama had asked me to journal, but I never would. Well, the stroke attacked my brain, but it also touched my heart. So after I learned how to write again, I tried journaling and I'm so glad I did. Even though I'm not able to work as a nurse right now, I know I am still here to help others and gratitude will show me how, beginning with this book.

Don't wait until you get sick or get into trouble to be grateful. Start now. One day at a time, list ten things you're grateful for. Stick with it. You will see that it's like Mama said to me all along: the more grateful you are, the more reasons you will have to be grateful. My list keeps getting longer and longer. Thank you Mama!